OLIVE TREE

FORGIVENESS, PEACE AND PROSPERITY

ABOUT THE OLIVE TREE

The olive branch symbolizes peace and forgiveness in several cultures around the world. In ancient Greece the olive branch signified peace and prosperity while in the Roman Age an olive branch was offered to seek peace in times of war. There are several hypotheses regarding the origin of the olive branch representing peace.

According to one belief olive trees takes a long time to bear fruit and hence could be grown in times of peace only which may have resulted in them being associated with times of harmony and goodwill. Another idea is that after the Great Flood a dove released by Noah returned with an olive branch signifying that land was in sight and that peace was again descending on Earth.

Two theories on forgiveness: 1) once an olive tree begins growing, it's hard to kill, just as a person who has forgiven once can more readily do so again, and 2) just as a person needs a bath repeatedly, so we also need to forgive repeatedly.

Olive trees have long been cultivated for a variety of reasons. From their wonderful fruits and oils to their beauty in the landscape, they are truly a delightful addition to almost any environment. In most ways, olive trees are very forgiving to even the most inexperienced caretaker.

DROP THE
CHARGES

THE CONTINUOUS STRUGGLE WITH
OFFENCES & FORGIVENESS

* * *

AGNES MENSAH-BONSU

authorHOUSE®

AuthorHouse™
1663 Liberty Drive
Bloomington, IN 47403
www.authorhouse.com
Phone: 1-800-839-8640

Published by AuthorHouse   03/01/2012

ISBN: 978-1-4678-8989-6 (sc)
ISBN: 978-1-4678-8952-0 (e)

DEDICATION

* * *

This book is firstly dedicated to our Lord Jesus Christ who has left a prime example of forgiveness for us to follow.

This volume is lovingly and affectionately dedicated to my husband Reverend Henry Mensah-Bonsu who has made my home, ministry and entire life as heaven on earth.

The Archbishop Benson Idahosa of blessed memory & Bishop Mrs. Margaret Benson Idahosa of Church of God Missions International, Benin City, Nigeria, West Africa.

Also to our children; Miss Audrey, Kojo, Wiafe, Pops, Benson Mensah-Bonsu, Benjamin Osei Bonsu Ocran and Mrs. Becky Mensah for her loyalty to the Lord.

Apostle Carmen & Pastor Walter Lattimore of Victory Church Int. Fort Washington, Maryland, U.S.A. Rev. Dr. Christy Doe Tetteh of Solid Rock International, Ghana, West Africa.

CONTENTS

✳ ✳ ✳

Rev. Dr. Charles and Beryl Dixon of Charles Dixon Global Ministries, Miami, U.S.A. Rev. Dr Beatrice Ofosua of Universal Institute of Biblical Studies & Counseling, Montreal Canada. Bishop Charles & Prophetess Agatha Entsua (aka Fifi) of Prayer Palace International, Ghana, West Africa. Rev. Celia Appeagyei-Collins of Rehoboth Foundation.

Covenant People of Christ the King Dominion Place, UK. For your constant prayers, love and support.

To all who will understand and experience the dynamic life of forgiveness.

ACKNOWLEDGEMENT

*** * ***

This book is as a result of radio programs and preaching in local and international assemblies.

I therefore acknowledge Bishop James Saah, Action Chapel International; Rev. Mosy U. Madugba, International Head Coordinator of Minister Prayer Netwok. Apostle and Rev. Mrs Onyebuchi Daniel, President, Elohim Powerhouse Ministry International. Rev. Mrs Yinka John, Senior Pastor, Frontline International Church. Ms Katharine Ashong, Life Coach and Rev and Mrs Adu Sarpong, Ghana. Derick Agyekum Ansong and Ms Abyna Ansah Adjei, Ghana. Rev Godwin Oppong and Rev Gideon Akoto, Ghana. Ms Patricai Aidoo and Ms Kuria Amoyaw, London, for their intercessory prayers.

I also acknowledge the thousands of listeners, host ministers, countless believers and unsaved who have testified about the healing, deliverance, restoration and joy they have experienced through these teachings of Drop the Charges.

ENDORSEMENT

* * *

This book by Rev. (Mrs.) Agnes Mensah-Bonsu is a vital manual for all Christians. With simplicity and clearity Pastor Agnes has written a book that will challenge everyone - from the greatest preacher to the least person on the church pew! She has shown that UNFORGIVENESS is a spirit and has also revealed the ancestral connection to the problem. Pastor Agnes has exposed the virus called BITTERNESS. She has beautifully shown what forgiveness is not, and what it really is!! With relevant stories and moving testimonies Pastor Agnes has made it easy for everyone to grasp the message, return to the paths of righteousness and re-discover God's plan for them. This book will help prepare the Church for the coming revival and help believers make the necessary adjustment to go to heaven!!! I whole-heartedly recommend this book to the Body of Christ.

Apostle Onyebuchi Daniel
President, Elohim Powerhouse Ministry Int'l,
No. 1 Elijiji Rd./55 Woji Rd., Woji,
Port Harcourt, NIGERIA.

* *

Forgiveness; this subject is not commonly preached or taught in the pulpit today because it is a difficult thing to deal with.

Anyone who is courageous and bold enough to write on this all important subject of forgiveness is truly God sent.

From the highly walled castle and palaces of kings and queens from the offices of Presidents and mansions of the rich and famous to the little hut in the hamlets of villages of the poorest poor everybody needs forgiveness. We always offend and are offended.

Rev. Dr. Christy Doe Tetteh
Senior Pastor.
Solid Rock Chapel International, Ghana.

* *

I have personally sat under the teaching of Rev Mrs Agnes Mensah-Bonsu of the subject of forgiveness and seen the tremendous results the deliverance it brought to many people. I recommend this book on every bookshelf in homes and book stores. It is a must read.

The contents are rich and real. Be blessed.

As a Mentor, Spiritual Mother, Apostle, and educator of the Word of God Worldwide, I strongly recommended every pastor, leaders, men and women, boys and girls around the world to pick this wonderful book and your life will never be the same.

* *

Rev. (Dr) Beatrice Nana Ofosuah
Senior Pastor and Author of 7 Best Selling Books
Strong Tower Ministries - Montreal - City Canada

* *

Mama Bonsu, I commend you for listening to the divine leading of the Holy Spirit, in writing a book on the subject of forgiveness. This is a subject that God personally dealt with me on. Several years ago, my Senior sister offended me, I was so deeply hurt, that I did not speak to her for five years, all the family and her children try to beg to forgive her, I refused, because I believed that with everything I have been through because of her, she should be the last person to do what she did to me. Then one day I slept and God open my eye to see rapture; and I did not make it, and I saw several people that I know who did not make it as well. Then I ask the Lord, what was their offence, and the Lord told me, adultery, lying, backbiters, the list went on, then I said to the Lord, I did not do any of these things, why did I not make it, and the Lord said to me, UNFORGIVENESS! imagine my surprise, I said to the Lord I am not holding on to anybody, and he said, what about your sister?. When I woke up and I realized that I was dreaming, I went on my knee and ask God for forgiveness and I called up my sister and told her it is over that I have forgiven her.

* *

Children of God, unforgiveness can cost you your eternity, please the time is now, Drop the Charges. I recommend this book for every Christian and every home, this is a treasure that can be pass on to your generation to come. I bless the name of the Lord for given us a real treasure in the person of Rev. Mrs. Bonsu, I pray that the wealth of wisdom given to you by the Lord will never run dry.
Shalom!

Pastor Rosalind Phillips
Grace Of God Ministries International
House Of Glory (USA)

* *

'Drop the Charges' is both spiritually and mentally stimulating. In this interesting book, Rev. Mrs Agnes Mensah-Bonsu engages her readers by placing much emphasis on the need for people to be ready and willing to forgive the offenses of others. In my candid opinion making the effort to forgive those who do us wrong is the panacea for spiritual, mental, emotional, physical and psychological malfunctioning. This literary work is destined to be a spiritual classic. Reverend Agnes Mensah-Bonsu's commentary is powerful and practical and will leave every person who applies the principles advocated in this book with a great hope to succeed. I highly commend this book to everyone and pray that you will read it to be wise and practice it to be right.

* *

Dr. Frederick Mmieh (Senior Pastor)
Maranatha Ministries Christian Centre
Grafton Square, Clapham Common,
London.

* *

Rev. Mrs Agnes Mensah-Bonsu's insights are clear, simple and extreamly powerful. This book titled *"drop the charges"* will definatly help you turn around every area of your life, as you embark on the journey of forgiveness ... Yes! A must read ....
Kathie Ashong
LIFE COACH
(Ghana).

INTRODUCTION

✳ ✳ ✳

I had the opportunity to preach on a Good Friday in one of the Pentecostal churches in Ghana, West Africa. This was at the invitation of a dear sister and pastor in charge of Solid Chapel, Rev. Dr. Christy Doe Tetteh. It was on the occasion of her 50th birthday celebration and I was led by the spirit of God to share a message with the congregation on 'forgiveness'.

As the message unfolded, it became obvious that a lot of people were listening with a heavy heart: deep resentment, grief and pain had swelled up in their hearts over the years as a result of some offences in the past. Interestingly, people had issues bordering on forgiveness.

Many people were seen shedding tears after the message. About ninety percent of the congregation, including ministers and guest artistes, responded when I called people forward for ministry. The presence of the Lord was so strong that everyone began to confess one

offence or the other and asking for forgiveness. It was a lovely sight to behold as people hugged each other, exchanged apologies and asked for forgiveness from one another in a remarkable way.
A remarkable sign of total reconciliation.

There was healing, restoration, joy, peace and anointing flowing through the congregation. All of them identified with the saying of our dear Lord and Saviour Jesus Christ as He hanged on the cross exactly two thousand years ago on that sacred Good Friday: *"Father forgive them for they don't know what they are doing."*

The message had such an impact that people stayed on till the evening service. Some participants even referred to me as 'aduro wura' a term in the Akan dialect which means 'the physician.' A man of God had this to say: *"I saw the word like arrows piercing the hearts of the people. It was hard truth and that is the only thing that can set us free."*

Testimonies that poured in the following day were quite refreshing. Let me share some of them with you.

A young woman told me about the bitterness she had harboured in her heart over the years because of the unruly behaviour of her step-children. This woman was almost in tears as she made reference to a point I raised in my message, that: *"people should treat other people's children, step parents and step children as their own. Since children who grow up without parental love become bitter and have a tendency of becoming a nuisance to the community."*

According to her, the step-children were never content with whatever she did for them. They were so spiteful and ungrateful. So she decided to stop giving them food and was not on talking terms with them for a long time, even though they lived in the same house. This incident nearly ended her marriage; it brought confusion between her and the husband. However, she was touched by my life-changing message on forgiveness and decided to forgive her step-children. She offloaded the bitterness in her heart and gave peace a chance. This started a process of restoring the relationship between her and the husband.

Also at the altar, an elderly woman wept bitterly as she narrated the ordeal she went through for seven years after being accused of killing her own son. Her son had died tragically and, to add to her woes, she was accused by her family of bewitching and orchestrating his death. At her old age, she was insulted, mocked, and rejected by the very people she needed most - her own family, and the community. Naturally, she could not stand the embarrassment of people pointing fingers at her anytime she went out. So she became confined to her room, harboured so much bitterness and felt deeply offended. She lived in a state of bewilderment and reproach until she finally found solace in the message of forgiveness.

The old woman summed up her relief in a simple statement:

"I have been enlightened, given the grace to forgive and freed from the devil's clutches."

The message came as a timely intervention because this old woman could no longer bear the agony. This could easily have hastened her death. She dropped the charges so that she can travel this earthly journey lightly, with no excess baggage. Furthermore, a young man told me that the word on forgiveness had delivered him from a possible tragedy. He had developed some deep hatred for his father and was planning to kill him. The only reason why he had delayed his plan was that he was unsure of the probable consequences of his action. This is what he had to say:

> *"I was thinking of shooting him. But I was afraid to be locked up in jail. It was all in my heart."*

These testimonies mirror the horrible situations many people go through on a daily basis. Human as we are, getting offended is inevitable but the critical point is our approach or reaction to such situations. The consequences of some reactions have been disastrous. Some people have even lost their lives because of their resolve to, as it were; *pay someone back in his own coin*. Others have taken certain actions which they later regretted. Ultimately, such people realise - too late - *that by dropping the charges* and forgiving one another, they could have saved themselves from certain catastrophes.

This book aims at providing an insight into how to rightly deal with offences. It encapsulates Biblical and moral principles that seek to enlighten us on the essence of forgiveness. To the downhearted, it portrays the need to have a forgiving heart and the benefit thereof in Christ Jesus. Enjoy the read.

...Keep a fair-sized cemetery in your back yard, in which to bury the faults of your friends...

Henry Ward Beecher

THE SPIRIT CALLED OFFENCE

✳ ✳ ✳

WHAT IS OFFENCE?

OXFORD dictionary defines Offence as the act of upsetting or insulting. Offending has to do with wounding the feelings of, or displeasing another; causing someone to feel annoyed or upset. It is also a breach of law, rules, duty, propriety, or etiquette; an illegal act, a transgression, a sin, a wrong, a misdemeanor, a misdeed; a fault. Also, it can be defined as a stumbling-block; a cause of spiritual or moral stumbling; an occasion of unbelief, doubt, or apostasy, hurt, harm, injury, damage, pain, (inflicted or felt). A simplified definition of offence is an injury or wrong done to someone and thus causing an ill feeling. This spirit of offence took its place in the Genesis, right from the formation of the first family. It is one of the major reasons why the church has failed to win the world.

This is because the spirit of offence hinders Christians from contributing to the flow of God's work.

Also, offence is one of the insidious and deceptive kinds of bait Satan uses to make us vulnerable. It is an invisible barrier that gives us a victim's mentality.

For instance, you allow a close friend into your bedroom and the next moment, every Tom, Dick and Harry gets to know about the poor state of your bedroom. Obviously, you will feel betrayed.

Bitterness is more devastating than betrayal. It is internally what you do to yourself; it steals your peace, joy, calmness and your rest. Betrayal is external; what others do to us. Thousands survive betrayal and disloyalty easily, only few, if there is any at all, can survive the devastating effect of bitterness.

Many have developed strange diseases and ended up in institutions such as psychiatric homes, prisons and hospitals, because they refused to let go. They allowed their offenders to control their entire destiny.

"For to this you were called, because Christ also suffered for us, leaving us an example, that you should follow His steps"

1 Peter 2:21

There is an example left for us to follow by our Lord and Saviour Jesus Christ as He says in *(John 15: 20) that, if they did it to me they will do it to you*. A servant is not greater than the master.

Everything starts as a seed and it has the potential of growing or germinating and bearing fruits. Offences could generate the following fruits: hurt, anger, outrage, hatred, bitterness resentment, jealousy, strife, envy, tension, conflict and many more.

As a matter of fact, offence is bound to come every person's way but it is very essential to set oneself free from its trap. Joseph went through a lot of ordeals but he did not allow himself to be offended by them, neither did he fall prey to the enemy. There is not a single person who has not experienced this diabolic trap. It is also like being diagnosed with cancer and pretending it will be cured by itself or it does not exist at all. In that sense, one will be gambling with his own life.

Most assuredly, people who are offended don't even realise they are trapped, it is pathetic. The consequence of falling prey to offence can be very disturbing. It is not a sin to be tempted, even Our Lord Jesus Christ was tempted yet never sinned. Temptation only becomes a sin when one gives in to it.

> *"For we do not have a High Priest who cannot sympathise with our weaknesses, but was in all points tempted as we are, yet without sin."*
>
> *Hebrews 4:15*

Martin Luther made a profound statement that, "you cannot stop birds from flying over your head but you can stop them from building their nests in your hair."

You cannot stop people from offending you but it is your reaction that counts and makes the difference. We need to understand this revelation that, some people hurt others because they feel insecure, jealous or envious. You may be blessed with what they have longed for.

Jesus said, "Father forgive them for they don't know what they do" when He was on the cross. He knew the purpose of going to the cross; to save mankind. To the Lord, the Kingdom assignment is mightier and weightier than the betrayal of Judas, the flogging of the Romans, and finally His being handed over by the religious leaders. He did not let their attack and persecution deter Him. Neither did He stop pressing on. No one can make progress by looking back; imagine a driver who keeps looking consistently in his rear mirror whilst driving, it could lead to a disastrous outcome.

"But we speak the wisdom of God in a mystery, the hidden wisdom which God ordained before the ages for our glory, 8which none of the rulers of this age knew; for had they known, they would not have crucified the Lord of glory."

1 Corinthians 2:7-8

Those who handed Jesus over and crucified Him didn't have the slightest idea what they were doing. Misguided people are ignorant about the implications of their actions. God in his mercy has devised a way of prompting us when we go wrong and this is what has kept us going up till now.

Let us consider these scenarios:

Why would Cain kill his brother Abel? Both presented sacrifices to the Lord. Abel's was accepted but that of Cain was rejected. Could anyone blame Abel for his sacrifice being accepted? No! Absolutely no fault of his. However, out of envy and jealousy, his brother murdered him. Everyone has a Cain in his life.

> *"And in the process of time it came to pass that Cain brought an offering of the fruit of the ground to the LORD. 4Abel also brought of the firstborn of his flock and of their fat. And the LORD respected Abel and his offering, 5but He did not respect Cain and his offering. And Cain was very angry, and his countenance fell. 6So the LORD said to Cain, "Why are you angry? And why has your countenance fallen? 7If you do well, will you not be accepted? And if you do not do well, sin lies at the door. And its desire is for you, but you should rule over it." 8Now Cain talked with Abel his brother; and it came to pass, when they were in the field, that Cain raised up against Abel his brother and killed him."*
>
> *Genesis 4:3-8*

A 'Lot' you travel with, when you are not supposed to, could later cause strife and create division and tension in your home, life and the Church.

"Lot also, who went with Abram, had flocks and herds and tents. 6Now the land was not able to support them that they might dwell together, for their possessions were so great that they could not dwell together. 7And there was strife between the herdsmen of Abram's livestock and the herdsmen of Lot's livestock. The Canaanites and the Perizzites then dwelt in the land. 8So Abram said to Lot, "Please let there be no strife between you and me, and between my herdsmen and your herdsmen; for we are brethren. 9Is not the whole land before you? Please separate from me. If you take the left, then I will go to the right; or, if you go to the right, then I will go to the left."

Genesis 13:5-9

Beware of the 'Laban' who cheats and exchanges your wages ten times.

"Yet your father has deceived me and changed my wages ten times, but God did not allow him to hurt me."

Genesis 31:7

Your brothers, who sold you into slavery because you shared your dreams with them, could breed envy and hatred.

"Now when they saw him afar off, even before he came near them, they conspired against him to kill him. 19Then they said to one another, "Look, this dreamer is coming! 20Come therefore, let us now kill him and cast him into some pit; and we shall say, 'Some wild beast has devoured him.' We shall see what will become of his dreams!" 21But Reuben heard it, and he delivered him out of their hands, and said, "Let us not kill him." 22And Reuben said to them, "Shed no blood, but cast him into this pit which is in the wilderness, and do not lay a hand on him"--that he might deliver him out of their hands, and bring him back to his father. 23So it came to pass, when Joseph had come to his brothers, that they stripped Joseph of his tunic, the tunic of many colors that was on him. 24Then they took him and cast him into a pit. And the pit was empty; there was no water in it. 25And they sat down to eat a meal. Then they lifted their eyes and looked, and there was a company of Ishmaelites, coming from Gilead with their camels, bearing spices, balm, and myrrh, on their way to carry them down to Egypt. 26 So Judah said to his brothers, "What profit is there if we kill our brother and conceal his blood? 27 Come and let us sell him to the Ishmaelites, and let not our hand be upon him, for he is our brother and our flesh." And his brothers listened. 28Then Midianite traders passed by; so the brothers pulled Joseph up and lifted him out of the pit, and sold him to the Ishmaelites for twenty shekels of silver. And they took Joseph to Egypt.

29Then Reuben returned to the pit, and indeed Joseph was not in the pit; and he tore his clothes. 30And he returned to his brothers and said, "The lad is no more; and I, where shall I go?" 31So they took Joseph's tunic, killed a kid of the goats, and dipped the tunic in the blood. 32Then they sent the tunic of many colors, and they brought it to their father and said, "We have found this. Do you know whether it is your son's tunic or not?" 33And he recognized it and said, "It is my son's tunic. A wild beast has devoured him. Without doubt Joseph is torn to pieces." 34Then Jacob tore his clothes, put sackcloth on his waist, and mourned for his son many days. 35And all his sons and all his daughters arose to comfort him; but he refused to be comforted, and he said, "For I shall go down into the grave to my son in mourning." Thus his father wept for him. 36Now the Midianites had sold him in Egypt to Potiphar, an officer of Pharaoh and captain of the guard."

Genesis 37:18-36

Joseph's brothers devised a plan that, Joseph has been devoured by a wild beast. Check this revelation: Joseph was substituted with a lamb. Then, he could not die again.

Your siblings could drive you away from your father's inheritance, because you are not of the same mother.

8

"Now Jephthah the Gileadite was a mighty man of valor, but he was the son of a harlot; and Gilead begot Jephthah. 2Gilead's wife bore sons; and when his wife's sons grew up, they drove Jephthah out, and said to him, "You shall have no inheritance in our father's house, for you are the son of another woman." 3Then Jephthah fled from his brothers and dwelt in the land of Tob; and worthless men banded together with Jep thah and went out raiding with him."

Judges 11:1-3.

The Absalom who discredits and defames you

"After this it happened that Absalom provided himself with chariots and horses, and fifty men to run before him. 2Now Absalom would rise early and stand beside the way to the gate. So it was, whenever anyone who had a lawsuit came to the king for a decision, that Absalom would call to him and say, "What city are you from?" And he would say, "Your servant is from such and such a tribe of Israel." 3Then Absalom would say to him, "Look, your case is good and right; but there is no deputy of the king to hear you." 4Moreover Absalom would say, "Oh, that I were made judge in the land, and everyone who has any suit or cause would come to me; then I would give him justice." 5And so it was, whenever anyone came near to bow down to him, that he would put out his hand and take him and kiss him.

9

6In this manner Absalom acted toward all Israel who came to the king for judgment. So Absalom stole the hearts of the men of Israel. 7Now it came to pass after forty years that Absalom said to the king, "Please, let me go to Hebron and pay the vow which I made to the LORD. 8For your servant took a vow while I dwelt at Geshur in Syria, saying, 'If the LORD indeed brings me back to Jerusalem, then I will serve the LORD.' " 9And the king said to him, "Go in peace." So he arose and went to Hebron. 10Then Absalom sent spies throughout all the tribes of Israel, saying, "As soon as you hear the sound of the trumpet, then you shall say, 'Absalom reigns in Hebron!' " 11And with Absalom went two hundred men invited from Jerusalem, and they went along innocently and did not know anything. 12Then Absalom sent for Ahithophel the Gilonite, David's counselor, from his city--from Giloh--while he offered sacrifices. And the conspiracy grew strong, for the people with Absalom continually increased in number."

2 Samuel 15:1-12

The Ahitophel who conspires with our enemies and betrays us.

"Then someone told David, saying, "Ahithophel is among the conspirators with Absalom." And David said, "O LORD, I pray, turn the counsel of Ahithophel into foolishness!"

2 Samuel 15: 31

The Shemeis who curse you because of their lack of understanding of situations.

> "Now when King David came to Bahurim, there was a
> man from the family of the house of Saul, whose name
> was Shimei the son of Gera, coming from there. He
> came out, cursing continuously as he came. 6And he
> threw stones at David and at all the servants of King
> David. And all the people and all the mighty men were
> on his right hand and on his left. 7Also Shimei said
> thus when he cursed: "Come out! Come out! You
> bloodthirsty man, you rogue! 8The LORD has brought
> upon you all the blood of the house of Saul, in whose
> place you have reigned; and the LORD has delivered
> the kingdom into the hand of Absalom your son. So
> now you are caught in your own evil, because you are
> a bloodthirsty man!"
>
> 2 Samuel 16:5-8

Other Notable Points:

- Your close friends, who call you names, in times of trials and blame you for your calamities - Job's example.
- The Judas who betrays us.
- The leaders who bring false witnesses against you because of your faith. Then watch you stoned to death. (Acts 7)
- A group of people who undermine you to get your position.
- One who betrays your confidence
- One who becomes ungrateful
- One who despises you because of your past
- One who deserts you in times of crisis.

Which of these categories above do you fall in?

Daniel was taken captive to Babylon as a young man. He left his home, culture and people, served four dynasties with an excellent spirit, even with those who plotted against him to be put into the lion's den. The Bible never recorded that he was offended or bitter against anybody.

Naman's little maid was taken as a slave after her parents have been killed. As an orphan, she could have been bitter and even planned to poison her master, but she rather prescribed a channel of remedy to him.

> "Now Naaman, commander of the army of the king of Syria, was a great and honorable man in the eyes of his master, because by him the LORD had given victory to Syria. He was also a mighty man of valor, but a leper. 2And the Syrians had gone out on raids, and had brought back captive a young girl from the land of Israel. She waited on Naaman's wife. 3Then she said to her mistress, "If only my master were with the prophet who is in Samaria! For he would heal him of his leprosy."
>
> ### 2 Kings 5:1-4

The antidote to such offences is to release all of them for the sake of our own peace. "Jehovah Shalom" - peace in the Bible goes beyond the absence of conflict or strife. It includes wellbeing, blessing and harmony with God. Jesus as the Prince of Peace brings us Peace with God and the Peace of God, including wholeness and total well-being.

"Not to forgive is to be imprisoned by the past, by old grievances that do not permit life to proceed with new business. Not to forgive is to yield oneself to another's control... to be locked into a sequence of act and response, of outrage and revenge, tit for tat, escalating always. The present is endlessly overwhelmed and devoured by the past. Forgiveness frees the forgiver. It extracts the forgiver from someone else's nightmare."

Lance Morrow

ANCESTRAL OFFENCE

* * *

STORY OF ESTHER - HAMAN
HARBOURS ANCESTRAL OFFENCE

THERE are families who harbour ancestral offences from generation to generation. In our days, when I was growing up, there were these two families who were well known for their high reputation. Yet they could never make peace with each other; from great grandparents to grandparents, from parents to their children up to grand children. One dare not cross the property of the other. There was so much hatred and hostility between them. It was traced back to the fact that they had political differences in the past. One family orchestrated the death of most of the men in the other family. These things are still happening not only in the Bible.

The book of Nahum says there is nothing new under the Sun. Prejudice is a vicious evil and it is hereditary, passed down from generation to generation. The root of Haman's bitterness toward the Jews can be traced back to his family tree. He was a descendant of Agag, the Amalikite king whom Samuel finally killed. The Amalikites had remained bitter enemies of the Jews, and the feud had been in existence for a long time.

Haman became offended and filled with rage, when Mordecai refused to bow down to him. Mordecai refused to bow to Haman for two reasons;

1.   The act would be considered idolatry by the Jews.

2.   In no way did he want to show respect to an Amalekite, an avowed enemy of his people.

The name of God was not mentioned in this book yet His fingers are seen moving from page to page, working out His best plans behind the scene. *(Esther 3:1-15)*

1 After these things King Ahasuerus promoted Haman, the son of Hammedatha the Agagite, and advanced him and set his seat above all the princes who were with him. 2 And all the king's servants who were within the king's gate bowed and paid homage to Haman, for so the king had commanded concerning him. But Mordecai would not bow or pay homage. 3 Then the king's servants who were within the king's gate said

to Mordecai, "Why do you transgress the king's command?"
4 Now it happened, when they spoke to him daily and he
would not listen to them, that they told it to Haman, to see
whether Mordecai's words would stand; for Mordecai had
told them that he was a Jew. 5 When Haman saw that Mordecai did not bow or pay him homage, Haman was filled with
wrath. 6 But he disdained to lay hands on Mordecai alone, for
they had told him of the people of Mordecai. Instead, Haman
sought to destroy all the Jews who were throughout the whole
kingdom of Ahasuerus—the people of Mordecai. 7 In the first
month, which is the month of Nisan, in the twelfth year of King
Ahasuerus, they cast Pur (that is, the lot), before Haman to
determine the day and the month, until it fell on the twelfth
month, which is the month of Adar. 8 Then Haman said to
King Ahasuerus, "There is a certain people scattered and
dispersed among the people in all the provinces of your
kingdom; their laws are different from all other people, and
they do not keep the king's laws. Therefore it is not fitting for
the king to let them remain. 9 If it pleases the king, let a decree
be written that they be destroyed, and I will pay ten thousand
talents of silver into the hands of those who do the work, to
bring it into the king's treasuries." 10 So the king took his
signet ring from his hand and gave it to Haman, the son of
Hammedatha the Agagite, the enemy of the Jews. 11 And the
king said to Haman, "The money and the people are given to
you, to do with them as seems good to you." 12 Then the
king's scribes were called on the thirteenth day of the first
month, and a decree was written according to all that Haman
commanded—to the king's satraps, to the governors who were
over each province, into all the king's provinces, to destroy, to
kill, and to annihilate all the Jews, both young and old, little

little children and women, in one day, on the thirteenth day of the twelfth month, which is the month of Adar, and to plunder their possessions. 14 A copy of the document was to be issued as law in every province, being published for all people, that they should be ready for that day. 15 The couriers went out, hastened by the king's command; and the decree was proclaimed in Shushan the citadel. So the king and Haman sat down to drink, but the city of Shushan was perplexed.

Esther 3:1-15

Mordecai's refusal to pay homage to Haman enraged the petty leader so much that he decided to make the whole Jewish population pay with their lives. Word of their impending doom spread throughout the Jewish community. When he realised that the fate of his people hanged by the thread of Esther's relationship to the king, Mordecai appealed to the queen to act swiftly.

He asked her to do a courageous thing - to stand alone before the king. Rising to the occasion of her need, God granted Esther the wisdom to devise a strategy that would eliminate the archenemy of her people. She invited both Haman and the king to a banquet where the king had vowed to hear what was troubling the queen and grant her wish.

Meanwhile, Haman was thrilled at the invitation. But as he passed the insolent Mordecai, who again refused to pay him homage, his elation turned into infuriation. And at the advice of his wife and friends, Haman erected a gallows from which he planned to hang Mordecai. The reason is obvious - he was offended.

Eventually, God used insomnia to awaken in the king an awareness of Mordecai's past heroism that had once saved the king's life. To this end, he decided that Mordecai should be exalted. So, instead of putting a noose around Mordecai's neck, Haman was ordered to drape a robe of honour over his shoulders.

Haman arrived at the royal banquet, unhappy about the sudden reversal of Mordecai's fate. Little did he know what awaited him. At the table, Esther revealed the plot against her people. The king then asked of the perpetrator's identity, and Esther pointed her finger at Haman. In a sudden rage, the king sentenced the arch villain to be hanged. He was hanged on the very gallows he had erected for Mordecai (Haman took offence against Mordecai because he would not pay him homage. In the end, he and his ten sons were killed).

THE MESSAGE OF THE BOOK OF ESTHER

Though God is invisible, He is also invincible. As the hymn writer proclaimed, "Immortal, invisible, God only wise." That is the message of the Book of Esther. The invisible God who may appear to be absent is the invincible God who is working out His wise plan. That is not only true for a young woman and her people in ancient Persia; that's true for any one reading this book today. Go back to Esther and let your mind linger over the incredible reversal of fates, those of Haman and Mordecai. Never should we underestimate the invincibility of a person who is in the will of God. The enemy shall gather together, but if not by God, he shall fall for your sake. Let go of the trap set before you by the enemy. Let God fight your battle for you, vengeance is the Lords, He will repay.

> *For we know Him who said, "Vengeance is Mine, I will repay," says the Lord. And again, "The LORD will judge His people."*
>
> **Hebrews 10:30**

Trust in the Lord for He will vindicate you at the appointed time. God's invincible providence will turn everything around. Never ever try to deal with a child of God yourself. Hand him or her to God. God knows how He deals with His people. No matter the offence, allow God to deal with it.

> *... Touch not mine anointed, and do my prophets no harm.*
>
> *Psalms 105:15*

> *Dearly beloved avenges not yourselves, but rather give place unto wrath: for it is written, Vengeance is mine; I will repay, saith the Lord.*
>
> *Romans 12:19*

Ananias (Acts 9:8-15)

Ananias had the opportunity of being part of Saul's sophisticated ministry, but because of the bad things he heard about him, he built an offence out of it and lost his part in this great ministry. Offence gained roots in his mind and it took a larger part of him than being a partner of Paul (Saul).

> *"Then Saul arose from the ground, and when his eyes were opened he saw no one. But they led him by the hand and brought him into Damascus. 9And he was three days without sight, and neither ate nor drank. 10Now there was a certain disciple at Damascus named Ananias; and to him the Lord said in a vision, "Ananias." And he said, "Here I am, Lord." 11So the Lord said to him, "Arise and go to the street called*

Straight, and inquire at the house of Judas for one called Saul of Tarsus, for behold, he is praying. 12And in a vision he has seen a man named Ananias coming in and putting his hand on him, so that he might receive his sight." 13Then Ananias answered, "Lord, I have heard from many about this man, how much harm he has done to Your saints in Jerusalem. 14And here he has authority from the chief priests to bind all who call on Your name." 15But the Lord said to him, "Go, for he is a chosen vessel of Mine to bear My name before Gentiles, kings, and the children of Israel."

Acts 9:8-15

Let us learn from Ananias' lesson. Many have lost their divine connection to their destinies because of what they have heard about their destiny connectors. There are many occasions people have come to us and made statements like this: "I have kept my distance from you due to testimonies I heard, but since I came so close I have learnt you are the jewel in my crown. Offence will blind you, prejudice will isolate you.

The Bible admonishes us to take heed what we hear. Whatsoever pains, wounds and hurts that have been inflicted in you emotionally, socially, spiritually and physically, pray and ask for the grace of God to empower you to let go, for this will relieve you.

"He said to them, "Take heed what you hear. With the same measure you use, it will be measured to you; and to you who hear, more will be given."

Mark 4:24

The carnal mind goes on to think about these wounds, but the spiritual mind submitting to the Holy Spirit enables you to forgive. We should learn to forgive.

...The glory of Christianity is to conquer by forgiveness...

William Blake

3

THE KINGDOM OF GOD AND OFFENCES

* * *

I T is very important that we address this issue of offence before we can come into the presence of God with a clear heart and mind. The Bible says that, *if we harbour iniquity, the Lord will not hear us (Psalm 66:18).* Many are busy serving God with contaminated heart but it is a waste of time.

> *"Whoever receives one little child like this in My name receives Me. "But whoever causes one of these little ones who believe in Me to sin, it would be better for him if a millstone were hung around his neck, and he were drowned in the depth of the sea.*
> *Woe to the world because of offenses! For offenses must come, but woe to that man by whom the offense comes! If your hand or foot causes you to sin, cut it off and cast it from you. It is better for you to enter into life lame or*

maimed, rather than having two hands or two feet, to be cast into the everlasting fire. And if your eye causes you to sin, pluck it out and cast it from you. It is better for you to enter into life with one eye, rather than having two eyes, to be cast into hell fire."

Matthew 18:5-9

This is a hard saying from the Lord Jesus Christ. He says anyone who offends these little ones does not deserve to live. Offences are bound to come because we are human.

Jesus is saying here that, offences are inevitable and we cannot escape them. We are bound to offend one another; we are bound to step on one another's toe, either intentionally or unintentionally. We cannot help it. It is bound to come. But whoever is used as an instrument to bring these offences into being shall be in serious trouble.

Woe unto such a person, Jesus stated. But He also said that we should be alert and guided because our adversary, the devil, is roaring about like a lion looking for whom he may devour.

The devil will not come in any way visible because he is crafty and cunning. He will therefore use the person close to you. Anyone who avails himself to the devil will be used by him. Woe unto anyone by whom offences will come. Woe means to be judged, to be unhappy. Sorrows and misfortunes are pronounced upon that person.

"Give no offense, either to the Jews or to the Greeks or to the church of God."

1 Corinthians 10:32

"We give no offense in anything, that our ministry may not be blamed."

2 Corinthians 6:3

Jesus continues to say that His people will be divided and separated because of offences. Anyone who gets offended withdraws from the others. It is the devil's number one strategy to divide and bring factions around us.

It is said in *Proverbs 18:19,*

"A brother offended is harder to win than a strong city, and contentions are like the bars of a castle."

Many are playing it safe because of offences. They build walls around themselves and decide to let in only those they think they can trust. This is another way of opening doors to more hurt. Let us learn to trust the Lord.

JESUS WARNS OFFENDERS

Jesus is warning us about offences. He is so much concerned about His kingdom and the citizens. He loves them so much so that He says;

"Whoever causes one of these little ones who believe in me to sin, it would be better for him if a millstone were hung around his neck, and he were drowned in the depth of the sea.
Matthew 18:6

He who offends the people of the Lord offends the Lord Himself. He is part of His people and His people are part of Him. That is why He says that, when you do well to any of His people, you have done it to God. Whatever affects us affects Him as well.

The Three Parties

There were three opposition parties in Jesus' days. They were all around Him day and night, not because they loved Him and wanted to hear His teachings, but because they were there to pick up pieces of fault with Him and tried to oppose His work and teachings. These are Pharisees, Sadducees and the Scribes. The three religious groups tried to oppose Him. Because of their fault-finding nature, they had no stability in their life.

"Beloved does this ring a bell?

There are people Jesus said that in the last days many will be offended, will betray one another, and will hate one another."
Matthew 24:10

To His disciples, He said the following:

..."All of you will be made to stumble because of me

this night, for it is written: 'I will strike the Shepherd, and the sheep of the flock will be scattered."

Matthew 26:31

Offence - A Hindrance

Offence hinders our flow in life. Many people have left their place of calling into other uncalled positions because of offence.

Some are sitting on the fence and have become apathetic. These are not ordinary people but noble men and women who have been called as leaders and shepherds.

Some people left their ministry because they were offended and they were convinced by friends who seem sincerely concerned for their welfare and their own desires, believing that they had the capability to establish their own ministry and should not allow anyone to stand in their way. The greatest trap of the enemy is, believing his lies and deception.

Offences drive many out of God's will

Many people could not reach their destinies in life because of offences. These include trainees, apprentices, protégées in different trades, and even in relationships. Their decision to establish their own ministry, trade or business was premature, and some rush into another relationship to proof a point.

The moment we begin to lead God instead of allowing God to lead us, our ministries will not function well. Offences create a weak foundation; anything without a strong foundation has no future. It might hang on for a temporal period, just as Jesus said in Matthew 7:24-27:

> *"Therefore whoever hears these sayings of Mine, and does them, I will liken him to a wise man who built his house on the rock: 25and the rain descended, the floods came, and the winds blew and beat on that house; and it did not fall, for it was founded on the rock. 26But everyone who hears these sayings of Mine, and does not do them, will be like a foolish man who built his house on the sand: 27and the rain descended, the floods came, and the winds blew and beat on that house; and it fell. And great was its fall."*

Offences have caused broken relationships, which have separated ministers from ministers, pastors from congregation and brothers from one another, husbands from wives, parents from their children, families from each other, employers from employees, teachers from students, coaches from players and destroyed intimate long term friendships.

The Lord knows the heart of men and how weak we are, so He encourages us to study His word coupled with the sensitivity to the Holy Spirit and allowing Him to have His way. If the Word is not in you, you cannot endure and it will cause you to backslide or stumble. That is what offence does; to cause people to backslide.

THE WEALTH OF THE CHURCH

God has endowed His body with spiritual gifts that should be manifested among His people. Nevertheless, there are some aspects of our lives that hinder the manifestation of His glory. These cause us to withdraw ourselves from the Word of the Lord or close in to them, not being open up to receive from the Lord.

Notable among such hindrances is the subject in question *"offences"*
 As a result, the church has experienced more divisions among ministers and believers. Apparently, this kind of spirit affects not only congregation members, but also Archbishops, Bishops, ministers, elders, deacons.
Every Tom, Dick and Harry is caught up in it. Hence, it affects the wealth of the church.

The moment these things begin to move in the house of God, the Holy Spirit cannot manifest Himself and the anointing of God cannot demonstrate His power in His full capacity in our midst. When this happens, the Holy Spirit withdraws from us.

Offence has retarded the progress of the church of the Lord. When this spirit begins to move in the house of God, in the home, in the office, in the school, we make life miserable for others including new believers.

However, the only way to maintain the rich spiritual fabric of the church is to forgive and love each other as Christians.

How are we offended?

We harbour things that we hear about us in our hearts instead of taking the boldness and the courage to find out more. We nurture it and it grows and then we begin to dwindle because it starts to kill the spirit in us.

When you hear anything that has been said about you, ask! The most important thing to do is to find out if that which is been rumoured about you is true. Initiate the contact and confront the person in private. "You cannot conquer what you cannot confront." says Paula White. That is one way of dealing with this spirit of offence.

> *"Moreover if your brother sins against you, go and tell him his fault between you and him alone. If he hears you, you have gained your brother. 16. But if he will not hear, take with you one or two more, that 'by the mouth of two or three witnesses every word may be established.' 17. And if he refuses to hear them, tell it to the church. But if he refuses even to hear the church, let him be to you like a heathen and a tax collector. 18. Assuredly, I say to you, whatever you bind on earth will be bound in heaven, and whatever you loose on earth will be loosed in heaven.*
>
> *Matthew 18:15-18*

If we begin to practice this, the spirit will cease operating among us. Many a time, there is no element of truth in these charges but just to bring division, confusion and hindrances in the lives of the people. The ploy of the enemy.

"If your right eye causes you to sin, pluck it out and cast it from you; for it is more profitable for you that one of your members perish, than for your whole body to be cast into hell. And if your right hand causes you to sin, cut it off and cast it from you; for it is more profitable for you that one of your members perish, than for your whole body to be cast into hell."

Matthew 5:29-30

Imagine someone refusing to go to work because his supervisor has offended him or her. Such an individual could easily be dismissed or suspended for the deliberate absenteeism. But in the house of God, it is different. For example, a leader in the church can stop a particular work in the house of God when he or she is offended. A praise and worship leader or worker could refuse to lead because he or she has been offended. The same can be said of a member of the ushering team, financial committee member, men and women fellowship among others.

After speaking in one of the conferences in the USA, a lady walked up to me after the service, sounding very overwhelmed
This is what she had to say:

"I know you are God-sent; because I have not seen our pastor smile for some time now, but upon listening to the Word, I saw him laughing. The entire church has been witnessing heaviness and so much tension due to some offences. There have been so much hurts and wounds being nursed. Today, salvation has come to this house."

Many do not understand their stewardship to the Lord. They render their services to God as if unto man. When they are offended, the work of the Lord suffers. One dangerous thing about taking offence is that, it stops your blessing. It quenches your spirit.

Offence is a device of the enemy to deny people of their long awaited breakthroughs. The devil uses this diabolic spirit to sabotage them. That is the reason why the Bible describes the devil as crafty and subtle. We need to be extra vigilant and not give him room.

> *"Lest Satan should take advantage of us; for we are not ignorant of his devices."*
>
> **2 Corinthians 2:11**

The Offended Disciples

> *"Then Jesus said unto them, Verily, verily, I say unto you, except ye eat the flesh of the Son of man, and drink his blood; ye have no life in you. Whoso eat my flesh, and drink my blood, hath eternal life; and I will raise him up at the last day."*
>
> **John 6:53-54**

> *"But there are some of you that believe not. For Jesus knew from the beginning who they were that believed not, and who should betray him. And he said, therefore said I unto you, that no man can come unto me, except it were given unto him of my Father. From that time many of his disciples went back, and walked no more with him."*
>
> **John 6:64-66**

When Jesus said something about giving His body and blood to us to eat, the people became offended because they were soulish. They were not operating in the spirit. They saw His message as a 'hard saying' and couldn't grasp the meaning. In that sense, they became offended and followed Jesus no more. (We are not cannibals to eat your flesh, they might have said).

The things of the spirit are so heavy and so strong for anybody in the flesh. If you allow the Spirit of God, He will minister unto you to understand people and their attitude and behaviour. But if you close in, you will never understand. That disciple, who turned away, could not ask Jesus to explain what He meant by "eating His body and drinking His blood," after all, they are not cannibals.

When the truth is preached, many reject it because it becomes a hard saying to them. If you are not of the spirit, you will not accept the things of the spirit. People get angry because the truth has been spoken out. The carnal mind can never understand the things of God

> *"For what man knows the things of a man except the spirit of the man which is in him? Even so no one knows the things of God except the Spirit of God. 12 Now we have received, not the spirit of the world, but the Spirit who is from God, that we might know the things that have been freely given to us by God.."*
>
> **1 Corinthians 2:11-12**

"Then His disciples came and said to Him, "Do You know that the Pharisees were offended when they heard this saying?" 13 But He answered and said, "Every plant which My heavenly Father has not planted will be uprooted.."

Matthew 15:12-13

The imagery in this scripture conveys the fact that, once the roots grow, they draw strength and nutrients to continue to supply a reason for cracking through, even the most arduous defense. Offence is a powerful force that can cause mental, spiritual, emotional and physical cracks in the life of those who walk in it. You cannot live in offence and enter the blessing which God has prepared for you.

You cannot fully enjoy the blessing of the Lord if you are unable to walk in forgiveness, no matter what people have done to you. Offence is like a chain, once it wraps itself around you, the result is a downward trend.

It's like digging out an irrelevant thing that has been buried.

Paul talked of the root of bitterness and most times when you ask people what made them bitter, it sounds nonsensical. Yes, it is usually mundane things like dislike for people or expressing ourselves as if the other person is less than us.

"I just don't like her" or "Who does she think she is?"
"I can even do it better than she can".
"Why should he get this?"
"He does not deserve that position."

My dear friend, catch this revelation today as you read this passage; the hatred and opinion of men cannot stop the endorsement of God for you.

Why have you chosen to stop all your service to the Lord and withdrawn because people are talking about you? Which of them died for you?

You are under an attack because you have the ball. Whoever has the ball is a potential scorer. The devil does not burgle empty houses. He is after what God has vestered in you.

John 10: 10a.
"The thief does not come except to steal to kill and destroy".

...Resentment is like a glass of poison that a man drinks; then he sits down and waits for his enemy to die...

Nelson Mandela

4

THE UNFORGIVING SPIRIT

* * *

A FOREIGN SPIRIT IN THE CHURCH

The unforgiving spirit has gained roots in the body of Christ and it is spreading its tentacles from the greatest to the least of us. Men and women of God have been caught up in this unfortunate situation. It is not uncommon to find Christians picking up unnecessary quarrels with each other, even in church. This situation is affecting the work of God and given the devil a leeway to operate. It is a hideous sin which could hinder the glory of God.

The coming of Christ is eminent and He is coming for a prepared bride without spots and without wrinkles. We need not be ignorant of the devices of the devil; this spirit is ruling many lives. This has affected the society, communities, homes, hospitals, schools, etc.

It is robbing us of our blessing, calmness and peace. This spirit of unforgiveness has separated parents from children and husbands from wives and has brought so much animosity among siblings. Intimate friends, who used to do things together, are now enemies.

This spirit starts as a seed of resentment, germinates into revenge and grows into a deep root of bitterness. That tenaciously wrap around the heart until it becomes a cancer of hate for the offender. Never under estimate the diabolic nature of revenge.

The devil is using this spirit to cause many to dwindle. It has affected many spiritually, physically, psychologically, (emotionally) and has landed many in some confinements (mental homes, prisons and hospitals)

Can the Jews forgive the Germans?

Many years ago, I was invited to preach at an 'all night' service in a local church. I was given two months advance notice to prepare. I already had a message in mind but decided to wait on God for more anointing and direction. In due course, the Lord showed me the appropriate message to minister to the people. The provident God showed up in a unique and strange manner. I felt a tap on my shoulder and I heard one simple word "Forgiveness." I had to go through the Bible and prepare a message in that direction.

On the day of sharing the message, the place was packed with hungry souls. In the middle of the message, people could not hold back their emotions as tears strolled down their faces. Then I understood why the Lord gave me that message. Many hearts were touched as I began to give Biblical examples to buttress my points, particularly on the need for us to forgive. A notable example was how David forgave King Saul and even spared his life when he had every opportunity to kill him. This was a man who had wanted to eliminate David. Faced with this situation, many people would not have wasted time in eliminating their enemies. But, it doesn't work that way because vengeance is of the Lord. There is this saying, whosoever knows how to fight his own battle does so without Divine interruption.

A young lady in the congregation, who could no longer contain her anxiety and anger, jumped up and exclaimed, "You mean the Jews should forgive the Germans?"

I answered, "Yes, as the Bible says in **Matthew 6:14**"

> *"For if you forgive men their trespasses, your heavenly Father will also forgive you". When you sow forgiveness, you reap the same from the Lord.*

This young lady, who was engulfed in tears, proceeded to the altar to share her experience after the ministration. She had been abused by her father and this had haunted her for years. The grace of God abounded on her and she was delivered.

The Holy Spirit manifested himself so strong in that place and there was so much emotional healing. Everybody began to confess offences and asked for forgiveness. Many reconciled with relations, after many years of separation.

A Testimony of Great Deliverance

One of the leaders of the church was also caught in the same trap of bitterness. She was expecting a baby and her condition made her go through so much stress. This prevented her from discharging her duties.

A couple of weeks later, we received a phone call that she had delivered a baby. On the day of our visitation, she gave an astonishing testimony in the presence of the husband. She and her husband had fallen apart since the beginning of the pregnancy. She went in labour with this grudge against the man. As a result of this, she went to the hospital alone without informing the husband. This was a great woman of intercession with a prophetic insight.

According to her, the pains became so intense and unbearable and time was running out on her. For days, she prayed and called on the Lord to intervene. The Lord told her to call up her husband or He would take her life. The spirit of the Lord then reminded her of the message of forgiveness that was preached on that Friday night.

At that point, she reluctantly called her husband. They had not spoken to each other for almost seven months, even though they lived under one roof. On his arrival, they held their hands and she delivered safely. She shared this profound testimony in the presence of her husband. This also blessed me for being attentive to the Holy Spirit.

What is more painful than doing right and suffering wrong, to kill the spirit within you, as people inflict wounds in you? There is deliverance in forgiveness.

You may be in the same situation and find it very difficult to drop the charges against an individual, a parent, child, a spouse or an ex, a minister of the gospel, congregation member, a sibling, an auntie, an uncle, teacher, a doctor, a close friend, a neighbor, a lawyer, the travel agent, an accountant, dress maker, employer, the landlord, the list is endless.

Would you choose death instead of forgiveness? The woman of God nearly lost her life and probably her unborn baby. Let this testimony be a turning point for you. Life is worth living. Jesus loves you.

> *"The merciful man does good for his own soul, But he who is cruel troubles his own flesh". Do not be your own enemy."*
> **Proverb 11: 17,**

CAUSES OF UNFORGIVENESS

There are a lot of factors that cause people to fall into this trap. Many of us decide not to forgive when we find ourselves in the following situations:

Wounded: An injury to the body in which the skin or a tissue is broken, cut, pierced, torn, etc.

Abused: To hurt by treating badly; mistreat

Falsely Accused: To blame wrongly

Bruised: An injury to one's feelings, spirit, etc.

Betrayed: Be a traitor to; to reveal unknowingly or against one's Wishes.

Cheated: The most general term in this comparison, implies dealing dishonestly or deceptively with someone, to obtain some advantage or gain.

Defrauded: Chiefly a legal term, stresses the use of deliberate deception in criminally depriving a person of rights or properties.

Duped: Stresses credulity in the person who is tricked or fooled.

Hoaxed: Implies a trick skillfully carried off simply to demonstrate the gullibility of the victim.

Undermined: Damaged, diluted, destabilized.

Swindled: Stresses the winning of a person's confidence in order to cheat or defraud that person of money, etc.

Tricked: Implies a deluding by means of a ruse, stratagem, etc. but does not always suggest fraudulence or a harmful motive

Hated: Implies a feeling of great dislike or aversion, and, with persons as the object, connotes the bearing of malice.

Humiliated: To hurt the pride or dignity of, by causing to be or seem foolish or contemptible.

Rejected: To discard or throw out as worthless, useless, or substandard; cast off or out to deny acceptance, care, love, etc. to (someone).

Slandered: Insult, defame, malign, smear, slur.

Disappointed: Disillusioned, upset, let down, dissatisfied, frustrated.

> *"If you forgive others the wrongs they have done to you, your Father in heaven will also forgive you. But if you do not forgive others, then your father will not forgive the wrongs you have done."*
>
> **Matthew 6:14, 15**

I would share some of these things I have learnt about forgiveness later on and expose the parables of forgiveness; what forgiveness is not and what forgiveness truly is. Once we understand these two sides of the coin, we can start to make true progress in forgiving.

...Forgiving does not erase the bitter past. A healed memory is not a deleted memory. Instead, forgiving what we cannot forget creates a new way to remember. We change the memory of our past into a hope for our future...

Louis B. Smedes

5

WHY ARE YOU BITTER?

* * *

Many years ago, I read in one of the newsletters of Dr. Yonggi Cho's church, Full Gospel Central Church in Ahido, South Korea, of a man who had gone to fight for his nation during the Korean War.

While in battle, he had signed all his salary over to his wife. He agreed that once he was back he would resign from the army and with all the money she was saving on their behalf; he would buy a house and settle down to a civilian life.

Five years later, he wrote to his wife to inform her about his coming back. As he arrived from the battle, there was no one to meet him at the airport. He took a taxi to their old home only to be told she no longer lived there. He searched for her everywhere and finally heard she had married someone else and gone off with the money. When he turned to his in-laws to complain, they beat him and kicked him out. He became very bitter with himself, God, his wife, the system and everyone.

In the end, he had intestinal damage and internal hemorrhage. He could not be cured. People directed him to Dr. Yonggi Cho for prayer and healing. As he stood before the man of God to be prayed for, the Spirit of God told Yonggi Cho to ask the man to forgive his wife. His response was "a big resistance." He then went ahead to narrate his story to the man of God. You see, bitterness puts people into rage, frustration and bad memories.

Dr. Paul Yonggi Cho went ahead to let him know that unless he forgave his wife and declared with his mouth that he loved his wife, he could not be healed and made whole. It sounded like an insurmountable mountain but once he began to see reason and obeyed, his courage increased and I believe the Holy Spirit gave him more strength. In no time he became healed and a strong supporter of the ministry of Dr. Cho.

Bitterness results in hurt and possibly fits of rage, epilepsy and other psychological problems. It can kill one physically and emotionally. Bitterness limits your vision, your scope and ability to reason.

> "Come now, and let us reason together," Says the LORD, "Though your sins are like scarlet, They shall be as white as snow; Though they are red like crimson, They shall be as wool."
>
> **Isaiah 1:18**

Bitterness is something that people could easily deny in their life until they come face to face with persons who offended them.

CONSEQUENCES OF BITTERNESS

1. Bitterness makes you walk in unforgiveness. As a result, you cause your prayers not to be answered.

    "Be angry, and do not sin": do not let the sun go down on your wrath."

    Ephesians 4:26

2. Walking in bitterness releases toxins into your body system. This causes sickness and diseases to come upon you. Releasing the offender from your mind and heart will cause your healing.

    Resentment is like a glass of poison that a man drinks; then he sits down and waits for his enemy to die

    Nelson Mandela

    Once you are in a state of bitterness, the people you are bitter about don't even need to be present to control you. One unconsciously or consciously hands over his entire live to the offender.

Bitterness prevents you from heaven's blessing since you have refused to give earthly forgiveness. Bitterness is like handing over your next access to the blessing of God; your ticket to the favour of God. Inadvertently, you hand over your destiny to the people about whom you are offended.

Bitterness exposes you to tumours, headaches, pains and pressures. It exposes your body to sicknesses and diseases. This happens because you have denied yourself the benefits of the covenant.

Bitterness could make you rejoice in iniquity. It makes you wish for bad things to happen to your offenders. When you walk in bitterness your theology becomes unbalance, you cannot quite understand why God has not killed all those who offended you and if they prosper at such times, it makes you question God's wisdom. It is as if God has chosen to partner with those you consider your enemies. Bitterness makes your life an open, incurable sore which is perpetually exposed until other destructions come in. People's spiritual statuses do not preclude them from bitterness.

It has been known that sometimes great Bible teachers, prayer warriors, great psalmists, and people we hold in high esteem, have become angry and misbehaved publicly when they saw someone who had offended them.

Breaking Free From Bitterness

Choose Blessing, Not Bitterness
Some people's reaction to life is that, bitterness is almost incurable, giving the impression that they cannot react differently to situations. A good number of people who have chosen to bless and not be bitter in Scripture had the toughest of experiences.

Imagine the case of Esau whose birthright was taken by Jacob and his blessing passed on to Jacob. Esau vowed to kill Jacob after the death of their father.

> *"But Esau ran to meet him, and embraced him, and*
> *fell on his neck and kissed him, and they wept."*
>
> ### Genesis 33:4

When they met twenty years later, Esau's heart had healed. He forgave Jacob and God blessed him. Unfortunately, some people can harbour bitterness in their hearts for decades.

1.   PEOPLE WHO WALKED IN BITTERNESS

Cain was the first son of Adam, and possibly the twin brother of Abel. He got it all wrong when God blessed the offering Abel gave. His reaction is at the root of many people's bitterness - Envy! Once they cannot fathom why some people are blessed, they become bitter and tend to blame God. They easily wish evil for such people.

Bitter people find it difficult to comprehend when certain men and women walk in favour, though they seem undeserving. They cannot simply come to terms with what exactly favour is.

A bitter man cannot understand why in your season of 'open-doors' things just seem to work for you.

"And in the process of time it came to pass that Cain brought an offering of the fruit of the ground to the LORD. Abel also brought of the firstborn of his flock and of their fat. And the LORD respected Abel and his offering, but He did not respectCain and his offering. And Cain was very angry, and his countenance fell. So the LORD said to Cain, "Why are you angry? And why has your countenance fallen?"

Genesis 4:3-6

Bitterness caused Cain's countenance to fall and made him angry: because his brother's offering was accepted and the favour upon his brother was clearly manifest.

Precious one, any time you feel envious or jealous, please deal with it seriously in private, before it deals with you publicly. What you fail to deal with now is an accident waiting to confront you in future.

2.   THE BETRAYAL OF JESUS

"When Jesus had spoken these words, He went out with His disciples over the Brook Kidron, where there was a garden, which He and His disciples entered. And Judas, who betrayed Him, also knew the place; for Jesus often met there with His disciples. Then Judas, having received a detachment of troops, and officers from the chief priests and Pharisees, came there with lanterns, torches, and weapons. Jesus therefore, knowing all things that would come upon Him, went forward and said to them,

"Whom are you seeking?" They answered Him, "Jesus of Nazareth." Jesus said to them, "I am He." And Judas, who betrayed Him, also stood with them. Now when He said to them, "I am He," they drew back and fell to the ground."

John 18:1-6

Judas became bitter and in due course, betrayed Christ. It cost him dearly. He lost his bishopric. It cost him dearly because I am sure when we finally get to heaven, the Bible talks about the New Jerusalem, that it has twelve gates and the gates are in the name of the twelve apostles of Christ.

Thirty pieces of silver and a bitter spirit made him lose out on the opportunity to have his name cast, not in stone, but in gemstone.

3. THE PRODIGAL SON'S OLDER BROTHER

"Now his older son was in the field. And as he came and drew near to the house, he heard music and dancing. So he called one of the servants and asked what these things meant. And he said to him, 'Your brother has come, and because he has received him safe and sound, your father has killed the fatted calf.' But he was angry and would not go in. Therefore his father came out and pleaded with him. So he answered and said to his father, 'Lo, these many years I have been serv-ing you; I never transgressed your commandment at

any time; and yet you never gave me a young goat that
I might make merry with my friends."

Luke 15:25-29

The prodigal son's older brother is one of the most peculiar characters of the New Testament. He is not often referred to by people. However, his story reveals to us a man with a bitter spirit who had no capacity for giving or receiving forgiveness.

In his opinion, the favour and blessing were too much to be given to his sibling. His feeling was that, his brother did not deserve the forgiveness and acceptance he received after being such spendthrift.

The older brother measured everyone by his own standard and since he only expected a goat from his father, whoever had an ambition, vision, or desire for blessing that was greater than his was met with extreme bitterness. Bitter people do not take time to know the price you paid yet they cannot stand the prize you got.

This elder brother was in the house, he never left home. He reminds us of the type of people found in church who find it difficult to understand why God blesses new converts and younger ones. And why God blesses the seed that fell by the wayside. In their opinion, the man who backslid and finally came back home should be made to go to the bottomless pit of hell before he is finally accepted. They are so angry that they stay away from where you live or where you move.

Coming back to the story of the prodigal son, the Scriptures say the elder brother refused to enter when he heard the sound of music. Bitter people do not know how to rejoice with those who are rejoicing. Rejoice with those who are rejoicing, weep with those who are weeping. I will mention two more people who were bitter because they were turned down, rejected or had their counsel shunned.

AHITOPHEL

Ahitophel was a wise man, gifted by God. He was counsellor to King David; he was like the ears and eyes of the King. He harboured bitterness against the king, for David had taken his granddaughter Beersheba as wife after having her husband killed. Ahitophel waited for an opportunity to get even. He joined the rebellious son of the king and conspired against him. Having made a mistake by turning to counsel Absalom, he could not stand his counsel being rejected so he hanged himself.

> *"Now when Ahithophel saw that his advice was not followed, he saddled a donkey, and arose and went home to his house, to his city. Then he put his household in order, and hanged himself, and died; and he was buried in his father's tomb".*
>
> **2 Sam. 17: 23**

Let us resonate this in our spirit: God has a way of dealing with His leaders and people. The Bible says in *Romans 12: 19*,

> *"Beloved, do not avenge yourselves, but rather give place to wrath; for it is written, "Vengeance is Mine, I will repay," says the Lord.*

How about Absalom himself? He also died by hanging. These precious men allowed their bitterness to destroy them.

...When we forgive evil we do not excuse it, we do not tolerate it, we do not smother it. We look the evil full in the face, call it what it is, let its horror shock and stun and enrage us, and only then do we forgive it...

Louis B. Smede

6

THE ENEMY WITHIN

* * *

IN his book, Loyalty and Disloyalty, Dr. Dag Heward-Mills said he read a story of an Army General who surrounded a large city with the aim of conquering it. The city he attacked was heavily fortified with a high and imposing wall and gate. The army surrounded the city in readiness to attack.

One friend of the General came along and asked him, "Sir how do you think you are going to overcome the defences of this city? No one in recent history has been able to conquer this great city". The Army General smiled and said, "It's my fifth column. I am depending on them to do the trick." The General's friend was very interested and so he asked, "what is this fifth column? I thought you only had four columns." The Army General replied. "I do have a fifth column."

"Oh, I see, is it a special commando unit or are there airborne paratroopers." The man asked.

The General laughed and replied, "My fifth column consists of my spies, agents, friends and supporters who are already within the city. You just wait, they will open this gate from within and my army will rush in."

This is the only way the enemy can come in and destroy the family, the church, and the nation. David made mention of the enemy.

> *12 For it is not an enemy who reproaches me; Then I could bear it. Nor is it one who hates me who has exalted himself against me; Then I could hide from him. 13 But it was you, a man my equal, My companion and my acquaintance. 14 We took sweet counsel together, And walked to the house of God in the throng.*
>
> ***Psalm 55:12-14***

There are some who discredit their church, leaders, parents, husbands, wives, brothers, sisters and friends, among others, for this one reason - offence.

I would like to draw our attention to this cardinal truth, the devil's strength and power lies in his deception and lies.

FIGHTING THE ENEMY WITH HIS OWN WEAPON

It is a sin against God to refuse to forgive, regardless of the magnitude of offence. To make warfare more effective, don't conduct it with the devil's own weapon. You automatically lose the fight to him.

The film, *"Terminator"* featured a robot which detected anything made of metal and could assimilate anything. As a result, any attempt to deploy a metal weapon to destroy him was ineffective. Anything metal, he simply absorbed.

The Lord has given us His Spirit to demonstrate His power to bring healing and deliverance, restoration, joy, peace, rest and hope so that His name will be exalted and the lost will be won to His kingdom.

But when the lost is won in the kingdom, an offensive attitude drives the person back to his or her former place. It is an indirect way of telling that person that he is not needed in the fold. And he who is offended tries to offend others. It does not give glory to God, but rather stops the progress of God's work.

A WORD OF ADVICE TO LEADERS

I would like to admonish all of us to be aware of the people we put our trust in, and confide in with our secrets and confidence. This is where we meet betrayal, and this breeds wounds and hurts which makes forgiveness difficult.

One man of God shared his story with us some time ago. According to him, he had a very close friend in his church for years. Because he trusted this friend so much, he shared all his secrets with; he told him about everything that transpired in the church. Eventually, the pastor's private life became the talk of the congregation. This made him lose respect from his own members.

There was so much division and confusion in the church, which raised much concern.

I will strongly advise all who are in leadership not to forge intimate friendships in the church, college, or the office with your subordinates and share deep secrets with them. This man of God had to resort to prayer and fasting to resolve the issue. In the end, the devil was exposed, as happened in the book of Esther.

When Haman plotted to annihilate the whole Jewish race, because Modicai refused to bow to him as a god, Esther and the whole Jewish race declared a fast. The gallows built to hang Mordecai were eventually used to hang Haman.

The man of God stood in prayer and after the fast, the cause of the whole plot was exposed. His close friend had been divulging every secret and even exaggerating and fabricating stories about him in order to make the congregation bitter and lose trust in him. Some of them believed those lies and left the church anyway.

> *"Where there is no wood, the fire goes out; And where there is no talebearer, strife ceases. 21As charcoal is to burning coals, and wood to fire, So is a contentious man to kindle strife. 22The words of a talebearer are like tasty trifles, And they go down into the inmost body."*
>
> ***Proverbs 26:20-22***

God used this to teach the man of God a lesson. Yet, he had no right to be bitter against the brother. Even though, this nearly cost him his marriage of twenty-one years and a split in the Church.

Everyone of us has a weakness. There is no perfect man on earth, but if we can keep the matters of our hearts, share and pour them out to the Lord, it will save us a lot of trouble and disappointments. Some of these pitfalls could be avoided. Do not give room to the enemy.

Churches split, marriages go on rocks, families are divided, and the love of many has suffered due to words launched in bitterness and anger. Even though one might have a legitimate reason, the motives are not pure.

There are some individuals who can and have the anointing of fabricating issues. This can dampen one's spirit and it will only take divine intervention to heal and make such a person whole.

We have suffered many of these and have been victims up till this day. However, one secret we have learnt is that, the more we let go of these things the more doors God opens for us and makes us victors.

The Word and Spirit of the Lord has thought us how to endure and overcome these ploys of the devil. I must admit it has not been easy to let go, but by the grace of God, we have been able to let go and dropped all the charges.

We are free from Satan's trap and have our peace, joy and calmness of heart.

...Never does the human soul appear so strong as when it foregoes revenge, and dares forgive an injury...

E. H. Chapin

7

THE ACT OF FORGIVENESS

* * *

WHAT IS FORGIVENESS?

G ENERALLY, forgiveness means pardon, amnesty, exon-
eration, absolution, and acquittal, and remission,
absence of malice or grudges, mercy. It actually means
"letting it go", not holding anger or resentment against somebody who has wronged you.

When someone hurts or offends us, God says we should forgive.
Hit the delete button, just as you make a mistake when typing on
the computer and hit the delete button. Until you click the 'undo'
button, it is erased for good as if you never typed those words.
You may not easily understand why you need to forgive but one
thing I am certain about is that, it is for your own good.

Many years ago, it was reported in the papers that a man had divorced his wife and abandoned his four children for his mother in-law. Apparently, the woman's husband and the mother had been having a secret affair for sometime without the slightest suspicion. Can you imagine how the woman will react to this shameful biological mother of hers? How would she see her -mother or rival? How does she explain to her children? Is she their grandmother or step mother? Would this woman ever live to forget this hideous sin of her mother against her and her children? Yet the best for her is to forgive her and move on with her life, and let the mother live with this guilt.

A similar situation happened when a mother visited her daughter and her family in London ostensibly to take care of their new baby. The son in-law works in the night and the daughter in the day. Obviously, the husband and the mother were always in the house during the day time. Eventually, they began to have an affair. As destiny will have it, one day the woman had to come home unexpectedly. To her shock, she caught her mother and her husband in the act of sexual intercourse. She passed out and had to be treated medically. For days she could neither talk nor eat. It took months of counseling for her to get over the issue. She had vowed never to forgive both of them. By the grace of God she finally forgave her mother and the husband. Faced with these scenarios, many people would have taken a very uncompromising stance, no matter the seeming consequence. Many have murdered others in their hearts and minds.

Forgiveness unlocks genuine greatness. As a matter of fact, we do ourselves a big favour when we forgive. Bible affirms this in **Proverbs 11:17.**

> *The merciful man does good for his own soul, But he who is cruel troubles his own flesh.*

One of the typical examples I always share on forgiveness is about a story I watched on American talk show. It was about a mother whose only daughter was brutally murdered by a young man. To this end, the woman's only son also swore to avenge his sister's death. Eventually, the son ended up in prison for a different offence but he managed to work his way out to get transferred to the same prison where his deceased sister's murderer was. Apparently, this drew him closer to achieving his objective - to avenge his sister's death. However, the mother strongly admonished the son to let go and hand it over to God. This woman took her time to find out about the background of the young man who murdered her daughter. She then understood the circumstances or factors that led him to commit such an act.

The young man was an orphan who had been raised in a foster home and did not have the slightest opportunity to enjoy parental love, care and warmth. He was only stacked in an environment of hatred and struggle to survive.

The woman had pity on the young man, forgave him from her heart and even went ahead to visit him in prison and provided for his needs. She was able to convince her son to take the 'killer' as his own brother. To make the case more amazing, she filed in the court for adoption of the young man as her own son. Tears rolled in my eyes as the mother showed compassion and embraced the young man. This woman challenged many to forgive their offenders and move on with their lives. It was such a thrilling moment.

Faced with such a situation, many of us would have reacted quite differently. However, it is important to note that, refusing to forgive only piles up loads of bitterness in our hearts. It is just like the unexpected and expensive amount of money we pay at the airport if we carry more than the required weight.

The Bible says in *1John 3: 15,*

> *"He that hates his brother is a murderer and no murderer has eternal life in him."*

Since I became born again, I have seen this situation eat into the fabric of both believers and unbelievers. They always want to win the support and sympathy of other people against somebody because they have been hurt or bruised.

One of the examples many can emulate is that of the first black president of South Africa, Nelson Mandela who was imprisoned for almost three decades of his life for political reasons. Yet he did not keep record of the obnoxious deeds done against him, neither did he exhibit bitterness on a single occasion.

THE POWER OF FORGIVENESS

When we think of the word forgiveness, in our time, one of the names that come to mind is Nelson Mandela.

It is somewhat understandable to think of forgiving loved ones of minor offences against us, but it seems rather unimaginable to forgive people of atrocious offences committed against us.

Forgiveness can be defined as overlooking an offence, a transgression or a discourtesy, whereby the offender is exempted from paying the penalties for the offence or crime committed. But we find that no matter how deep seated the pain we have from past hurts, nothing compare to the healing and liberating power of forgiveness. Below are five truths you need to know about forgiveness.

1.   Forgiveness is part of the martyring process in life. It frees you from bitterness and the pain resulting from the hurt. As forgiveness traps you in the past, it locks up your ability to love people in the present and the future.

2.   It frees and heals all kinds of negative and destruction emotions i.e. guilt on the part of the offender and anger on the part of the offended. Lack of forgiveness sometimes leads to retaliation, which in turn brings the same guilt that the person who hurt you most probably feels. Other unhelpful emotions connected with forgiveness are extreme case of grief, anguish and depression.

3.   Forgiving others helps build and strengthen relationships. It is a virtue to be desired. The gesture of forgiveness removes the desire for retaliation and the display of animosity towards the offending party and hence creates an atmosphere for genuine love to grow.

4.   In my experience, I find that the most highly spirited people tend to be forgiving people - people who perhaps realise that no matter that sin or offence has been committed against them, they are capable of the same except for the grace of God. Infact, there is nothing quite like forgiveness that makes us quite like our maker. The reason Jesus commanded us to love our enemies and those who hurt us is in order that we may prove to be children of our God in heaven;

for He causes the sun to rise on the evil and the good, and sends rain on the righteous and unrighteous, Jesus clearly characterised His Father as one who loves even those who purposefully set themselves at enmity against Him.

That you may be sons of your Father in heaven; for He makes His sun rise on the evil and on the good, and sends rain on the just and on the unjust.
Matthew 5:45

5. Forgiveness frees you from the judgment of God. It is one of the ways to release the mercy of God. i.e. you cannot receive the forgiveness/blessing of God on a daily basis if you hold others in unforgivness *(Matthew. 6: 12 - 15)*

In conclusion, I pray that no matter your hurt today, that God, the Father of our Lord Jesus Christ, the Father of mercies and God of all comfort will comfort you in all your tribulations and challenges in life. I pray also that He who has the power to forgive will grant you love and grace to forgive those who have offended you.

What does our Lord say about this diabolic spirit?

> *"Then Peter came to Him and said, "Lord, how often shall my brother sin against me, and I forgive him? Up to seven times?" 22Jesus said to him, "I do not say to you, up to seven times, but up to seventy times seven."*
>
> **Matthew 18: 21-22**

Peter knew that he should not only bear grudge or meditate on revenge, but he was waiting on how many times he would have to forgive his offender. Maybe, at that time, some of the disciples had offended him up to a point that he wanted to retaliate.

The Lord answered him by saying, "Seventy times seven", which is four hundred and ninety times in one day. Who can offend one person that much in a day? The Lord therefore is telling us never to hold grudge. Forgive and drop the charges.

Whosoever loves his own soul will easily let go of the damage done against him. What we claim people have done against us is like a pin head compared to what we have done against the Lord

The Lord's Prayer

After teaching His disciples how to pray, Jesus knew that it is the tendency for man to retaliate when offended. The Lord, who knows the heart of man, taught the disciples about forgiveness in this prayer.

"And forgive us our debts, as we forgive our debtors."

Matthew 6: 12

In the teachings of the Lord's Prayer, this unpardonable sin is in black and white. If one does not forgive, he should not expect to be forgiven. One who fails to forgive is his or her own enemy in disguise.

"For if ye forgive men their trespasses, your heavenly Father will also forgive you: But if ye forgive not men their trespasses, neither will your Father forgive your trespasses."

Matthew 6: 14-15

What our fellow men have done to us is nothing as compared to what we have done against the Lord.

Forgiveness - A Human Struggle

The whole foundation of redemption is forgiveness. An act of God's grace is to forget forever and not hold people of faith accountable for sins they confess. To a lesser degree, it is the gracious human act of not holding wrong acts against a person.

Forgiveness has both divine and human dimensions (both vertical and horizontal). In the divine relationship, it is the gracious act of God by which believers are put into a right relationship with God and transferred from spiritual death to spiritual life through the sacrifice of Jesus.

It is also the ongoing gift of God without which our lives as Kingdom citizens would be "out of joint" and full of guilt. In terms of human dimension, forgiveness is that act and attitude towards those who have wronged us which restores relationships and fellowships.

David's Example

David expressed this terrible condition of the unforgiving sinner. In *Psalm 51*, David's first response following Nathan's confrontation is to claim God's grace.

> *"O God, According to Your loving kindness; According to the multitude of Your tender mercies, Blot out my transgressions"*
>
> **Psalm 51:1**

David knew that he was guilty and did not want to incur the wrath of God. So the king reached for his only hope of forgiveness - God's grace. What constitutes this grace? According to verse 1, it is a unique blend of God's loving kindness and His great compassion.

One classic illustration of God's gracious forgiveness is found in Psalm 103:12

> *"As far as the east is from the west, So far has He removed our transgressions from us."*

Have you ever tried going west until you found east? It's impossible! No matter how far west you go, you can still go further. The psalmist's point is simply this: When God forgives us; He places an infinite distance between our sin and us. People may tend to remind us of our past failures, but God completely removes them.

This same truth is also depicted in Micah 7: 19,

> *"He will again have compassion on us, And will subdue our iniquities. You will cast all our sins Into the depths of the sea."*

God could have kept all our shortcomings on a permanent file in heaven. Instead, He chose to bury them at the bottom of the sea. That is what is called grace.

Confess Your Sins

> *"Have mercy upon me, O God, According to Your loving-kindness; According to the multitude of Your tender mercies, Blot out my transgressions. 2. Wash me thoroughly from my iniquity, And cleanse me from my sin. 3. For I acknowledge my transgressions, And my sin*

is always before me. 4Against You, You only, have I
sinned, And done this evil in Your sight--That You may
be found just when You speak, And blameless when You
judge."

Psalm 51:1-4

Assured of God's grace, David then proceeds to humbly
confess his sins (Psalm 51:1-4). From his confession, we
can learn three helpful specifics to apply to our lives.

1.   **Call Them by Name**
     David was very candid about his sins. In verse 1,
     he calls them "my transgressions." In verse 2,
     David prays; *"Wash me thoroughly from my iniquity, and*
     cleanse me from my sin." He admits it as *"my iniquity"*
     and "my sin." In addition, he also portrays his sin
     with three pictures. In the first one, he portrays
     his sin as crime, asking for a pardon: "be gracious"
     (v. Ia). Secondly, as a debt, asking God to "blot
     [them] out"(v. 1b). And in the third, as a stain,
     asking God to "wash him thoroughly" (v.2).

2.   **Accept Full Responsibility**
     Notice also that David accepted full responsibility
     for his sin. He didn't come up with any elaborate
     rationalisations or attempts to shift the blame,
     "Lord, if it hadn't been for ..." He simply admitted the
     hard truth.

"Have mercy upon me, O God, According to Your loving-kindness; According to the multitude of Your tender mercies, Blot out my transgressions.2Wash me thoroughly from my iniquity, And cleanse me from my sin. 3For I acknowledge my transgressions, And my sin is always before me. 4Against You, You only, have I sinned, And done this evil in Your sight--That You may be found just when You speak, And blameless when You judge."

Acknowledge the cause and effect, Behold, I was brought forth in iniquity, And in sin my mother conceived me. (v. 5)

From the above text, David isn't saying that his mother was involved in a sinful act when he was conceived. Rather, he is saying that he received from his parents the same sinful nature all humans possess and passed it on to their offspring. David is acknowledging that the basic cause behind every sin is a nature that is "prone to wander, prone to leave the God I love," as the hymnist wrote. We can draw out another significant cause for David's sin from between the lines of verse 6: ***"Behold, You desire truth in the inward parts, And in the hidden part You will make me to know wisdom."***

For some time, David had chosen to forsake the truth and live according to his own sinful choices. What was the effect?

This is seen in what he asks God in verse 8. *"Make me hear joy and gladness, That the bones You have broken may rejoice."*

"Behold, You desire truth in the inward parts, And in the hidden part You will make me to know wisdom."

While David was unrepentant, his emotional health became weaker, taking his joy with it. Most likely, his unconfessed sin even took its toll on his physical health *(Psalm 32:3-4)*.

"When I kept silent, my bones grew old. Through my groaning all the day long. For day and night Your hand was heavy upon me; My vitality was turned into the drought of summer." Selah

3. **Construct New Patterns**
   David's thoughts shifted from correction to construction, beginning new patterns of living. This is affirmed in *Psalm 51: 10-12.*

OTHER NOTABLE LESSONS

Renew Me!

> *"Create in me a clean heart, O God, and renew a steadfast spirit within me." (v. 10)*

David asked God to create in him a clean heart, one that was completely different from the sinful one he received from his parents. What then happened to the old heart, the old lifestyle?

It is important to note that, when genuine confession is made, it is removed and buried; and in its place, God gives us a clean, fresh start. Following the confession, what did David need to nurture a clean heart? -"A steadfast spirit", meaning a disciplined mind that controls the emotions and guides the will to cleave to Christ and forsake sin.

Just as David reached up for a clean heart and a steadfast spirit, two fears suddenly threatened to stop him, fears that haunt those who abandon the Lord for an extended period of time.

The first was a fear that God will reject him, so David sought reassurance.

> *"Do not cast me away from Your presence" (v. 11a)*

David's second fear was that, God would withdraw His presence from him by taking away His Holy Spirit.

> *"And do not take Your Holy Spirit from me." (v. 11b)*

In verses *16-17*, we find that David's fears were allayed when he remembered God's merciful character.

> *"For You do not desire sacrifice, or else I would give it; You do not delight in burnt offering. The sacrifices of God are a broken spirit, A broken and a contrite heart-These, O God, You will not despise."*

David's broken and contrite heart found rest in the tender, forgiving arms of his God.

Restore Me!
Once his fears had been voiced, David then followed up his plea for renewal with a request for restoration

> *"Restore to me the joy of Your salvation, and sustain me with a willing spirit." (v. 12)*

What needs to be restored? - Joy and submission. David yearned for the joy he once knew, the one which came from having a heart that willingly obeyed God:

Once you have *"claimed"* God's grace, confessed your transgressions, and constructed new life patterns, David says we should share God's mercy with others.

Teach Sinners

> *"Then I will teach transgressors Your ways, and sinners will be converted to You." (v. 13)*

David's experience made him know the ways of transgressors, their heartaches and fears. And he also knew how to bring such people to the Lord.

Praise God

Another way of communicating your change is by praising Gods.

> *"Deliver me from blood guiltiness, O God, The God of my salvation; Then my tongue will joyfully sing of Your righteousness. O Lord, open my lips, that my mouth may declare Your praise." (v. 14-15)*

For almost a year, this songwriter and musician had been silent. Now he's eager to dust off his instrument and pour out the songs of praise in his heart. Note that David first sought God's help in freeing him from the guilt of his past sins *(v. 14a)*.

Is your obedience to God motivated by guilt or grace? When you've sinned, do you feel that you have to perform a long list of religious acts for God to accept you back? People may require us to clad ourselves in hoops to earn their acceptance, but God never does. He simply desires a heart that is humble, willing to be used again, eager to sing His praises once more.

Remember the Offended

In a very real sense, we all have our own kingdoms made up of families, friends, work associates, and other relations.

And, like David, when we wander into regions of sin it offends others and brings them suffering. So David asked God for help concerning Israel, because he realised that the whole kingdom had suffered under the weight of his sin.

We must understand that the sins we commit does not always affect us alone but extends to those around us.

When Jonah chose to disobey God, by boarding a ship to go to Tarsish instead of Nineveh, the Bible tells us that God sent a strong storm against them. Not until he accepted his responsibility, the lives of all those on board the ship could have been at risk.

> *"Do good in Your good pleasure to Zion; Build the walls of Jerusalem. Then You shall be pleased with the sacrifices of righteousness, With burnt offering and whole burnt offering; Then they shall offer bulls on Your altar." (v. 18-19)*

Sinners cannot live rightly without God. Once you decide to live in sin, you become isolated from God. It only takes the mercy and grace of God for one to find peace and forgiveness.

"Forgiveness is another way of admitting, 'I'm human, I make mistakes, I want to be granted that privilege and so I grant you that privilege."

Philip Yancey

8

THE TRUE CONCEPT
OF FORGIVENESS

* * *

"If you forgive others the wrongs they have done to you, your Father in heaven will also forgive you. But if you do not forgive others, then your father will not forgive the wrongs you have done."

Matthew 6:14, 15.

I would like to share some of the things I have learnt about forgiveness. As mentioned in previous chapters, I will to expose the parables of forgiveness; what forgiveness is not and what forgiveness truly is. Once we understand these two sides of the coin, we can start to make true progress in forgiving.

WHAT FORGIVENESS IS NOT

Forgiveness is not forgetting

We are taught from an early age to "forgive and forget." However, this is often not realistic and is not valuable. It would be nice to be able to turn back the clock and erase the unpleasantness of our past, but it just isn't possible. The real trick isn't to forget the past, but to learn from the past and try to use it to help yourself and others, both now and in the future.

Forgiveness is not condoning

Forgiving doesn't mean that the past was okay or not so bad.
Even though we were hurt (it was painful, and it affected our lives), forgiveness allows us to deal with the past in a more effective manner that doesn't minimise the past, but rather minimises the effects of that painful past on the present and our future. It in no way denies, justifies, or condones the original harm done to us in the past.

Forgiveness is not absolution

Forgiveness does not absolve the perpetrator of responsibility for their actions. It doesn't let them off the hook. The reality is that, we cannot grant absolution even if we wanted to, that is the sole responsibility of God. And while only God can grant absolution, only the perpetrator can seek it. They are ultimately responsible for their own actions and must make peace with their own past, just as we must make peace with our past. We don't forgive others for their sake. We forgive for our own sake, and for our own peace of mind.

Forgiveness is not a form of self-sacrifice

Forgiveness is not pretending that everything is just fine when you feel it isn't. This is perhaps the most difficult concept of forgiveness, because the distinction between being truly forgiving and simply denying or repressing anger and pain can sometimes be deceptive and confusing. Putting a smile on your face and "looking nice" is not forgiving. In any situation, there are two things at stake: we either have to forgive or not, there is no halfway. And we must be careful to be honest with ourselves, if we are not ready to forgive, because in the long run it is better to admit to and deal with our inability to forgive than just to pretend to forgive.

Forgiveness is not a sign of weakness

Far from weakness, forgiveness is a sign of true inner strength. When we forgive we understand that we don't need our anger and hatred to protect ourselves. We don't need the pain as a crutch anymore. Forgiveness doesn't depend upon who hurt us, what they did or whether or not they are sorry for their actions. We don't forgive out of our weakness towards the perpetrator, but out of our own internal strength. Forgiveness is something that we do for ourselves. In our own self-interest.

WHAT FORGIVENESS IS

Forgiveness is a form of realism.

It allows us to see our lives as they really are, probably for the first time. It doesn't deny, minimise, or justify what others have done to us, or the pain that we have suffered. It does, however, allow us to look squarely at old wounds and scars and see them for what they are. And it allows us to see how much energy we have wasted and how much damage we have caused ourselves by not forgiving.

Forgiveness is a sign of positive self-esteem

It allows us to put the past into its proper perspective, stop throwing 'pity parties'. The party no one attends. We no longer identify ourselves by our past injuries and injustices. We are no longer victims. We claim the right to stop hurting when we say:

"I'm tired of the pain, and I want to be healed." At that moment, forgiveness becomes a possibility -- although it may take time and much hard work before it is finally achieved.

Forgiveness is letting go of the past. Forgiveness doesn't erase what happened, but it does allow you to lessen and hopefully eliminate the pain of the past. And more impor-tantly, the pain from our past no longer dictates how we live in the present and can no longer determine our future.

Forgiveness no longer wants to punish those who hurt us
It means that we no longer want to get even, or spend time dreaming of how we will make them suffer for what they have done to us. It is realising that we may never be able to "even the score" and that, even if we did that, nothing we do to punish them will help to heal us. It is discovering the inner peace that we feel when we just let go of the past and forget about thoughts of vengeance.

Forgiveness is moving on
Forgiveness is in recognising all that we have lost because of our refusal to forgive. It's in realising that the energy that we spent hanging on to the past is better spent on improving our present lives and our future. It's letting go of the past so that we can move on.

We all have painful incidents from our past. And at one time or another we have all made the mistake of trying to run away from the past. The problem is that, no matter how fast you run, or how far you run, the past has a way of always catching up on you. In that sense, forgiveness is a way of dealing with the past so that we no longer have to run. It allows us to deal honestly with our past and to heal the pain. It helps us to find the inner peace that can come only from changing our attitudes.

One man of God wrote on Forgiveness: How to Make Peace with Your Past and Get on with Your Life - That is what forgiveness is all about. It involves working through the unfinished business, letting go of the pain and moving on for your sake. You forgive so that you can finally get rid of the excess baggage that has been weighing you down and holding you back so that you can be free to do and be whatever you decide instead of stumbling along according to the script that painful past experiences wrote for you."

I have forgiven everyone that has ever hurt me and moved beyond my past. It wasn't easy and it took a lot of time, but I believe that the rewards I experienced were worth the **effort. Perhaps you should give it a try.**

Forgiveness - The Greatest Challenge

The greatest challenge most of us face in our lives is swallowing our pride and admitting that we were wrong. It's a tough duty to summon the courage to admit to others, and to God, that we fall short of our best intentions that we sometimes make a mess of things.

Confession

More important than self-esteem, it is human nature to miss the mark of perfection. It is also human nature to convince ourselves that we really don't have to confess our shortcomings to anyone else. After all, our delicate psyches and our self-esteem might be wounded if we focused on such **negative stuff.**

> *"But I say to you, love your enemies, bless those who curse you, do good to those who hate you, and pray for those who spitefully use you and persecute you"*
>
> *Matthew 5:44*

Yet, out of the bad news of sin and separation from God and neighbours emerge the good news of forgiveness and reconciliation. God's promise, as recorded in *Isaiah 1:18* and *1 John 1:7-9,* offers to those who truly seek forgiveness a complete cleansing of the soul.

Forgiveness Brings Healing *(Deliverance, Recovery and Restoration)*

God gives us a very basic message right from the beginning-**"FORGIVENESS."** All through God's word; from Genesis to Revelation, the message is **"FORGIVE-NESS.** Jesus came to forgive the sins of mankind. To show by example what Godly living is all about? "Forgive us our debts as we also **"HAVE"** forgiven our debtors."

We ask God for forgiveness for the wrongs we do, and we say in the Lord's Prayer, "Forgive us" as we **"HAVE"** forgiven those who sinned against us. In effect, we are telling the Lord that we**"HAVE"** forgiven the people who hurt us in life, just as we ask him to forgive us for the hurts that we also inflicted on others. Forgiveness is supposed to be part of our new nature, which we inherited the moment we got born again. Once we become a new creation, we are supposed to be different and yet so many born again children of God "refuse to forgive".

"For in the same way you judge others, you will be judged, and with the measure you use it will be measured to you."

Matthew 7: 2

How can we come seeking healing from an All-Forgiving-God and refuse to obey His Word. So many Christians I know have hardened their hearts and died, never receiving their healing or blessing. Some strictly refused to forgive even their own family members. Ignoring the basic principle of what Christianity is all about.

Forgiveness brings deliverance, healing and restoration

The Ten Stepping Stones to Forgiveness

1. Be open to the possibility of changing your beliefs about forgiveness. Recognise that forgiveness is an act of strength and will, not weakness.

2. Be willing to let go of being a victim. Choose to believe that, holding on to grievances and unforgiving thoughts is choosing to suffer. Find no value in self-pity.

3. Remind yourself that your anger and judgments can't change the past or punish someone else, but they can hurt you. The events of the past cannot hurt you now, but your thoughts about the past can cause you immense distress and pain. Recognise that any emotional pain you feel this moment is caused only by your own thoughts.

4.   See the value of giving up all of your judgments. It is no coincidence that the happiest people are those who choose not to judge and know the value of forgiveness.

5.   Recognise that holding on to anger will not bring you what you truly want. Ask yourself this question, "Does holding on to my justified anger really bring me peace of mind?" Anger and peace; judgment and happiness do not occur at the same time.

6.   See that there is no value in punishing yourself. Once you truly recognise that you're angry, unhappy thoughts about the past are poisoning your life; you will embrace forgiveness and know the meaning of love.

7.   Believe that, forgiveness means giving up all hope for a better past! Accept your past, forgive your past, and embrace the present and future with hope! There is no law forcing you to remain a victim of the past.

8.   Choose to be happy rather than right. When we stop trying to control others and focus instead on our own thoughts, we give ourselves the gift of freedom and peace.

9   Believe that you have the power to choose the thoughts you put into your mind. Perhaps the greatest gift we have been given is the power to choose loving thoughts rather than angry ones. Your mind is not a 'dustbin' that will remain unaffected by the trash you put into it. Treat it like a garden and it will blossom.

10.   Be willing to make 'peace of mind' your only goal and believe that, forgiveness is the key to happiness. Peace will continue to abound in our lives regardless of the chaos around us, if and only if, we make it our single goal.

Choose not to let outside circumstances or people decide your happiness. Anger, judgments and unforgiving thoughts make us suffer. Releasing them brings us joy. It is as simple as that!

...We are all on a life long journey and the core of its meaning, the terrible demand of its centrality is forgiving and being forgiven...

Martha Kilpatrick

A FIRST CENTURY ACCOUNT OF
FORGIVENESS

* * *

BACKGROUND

O UR first glimpse into this particular situation comes through a stinging rebuke written by the Apostle Paul in his first letter to the Corinthians:

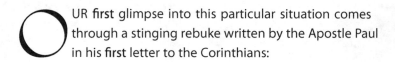

"It is actually reported that there is immorality among you, and immorality of such a kind as does not exist even among the Gentiles, that someone has his father's wife. And you have become arrogant, and have not mourned instead, in order that the one who had done this deed might be removed from your midst. For I, on my part, though absent in body but present in spirit, have already judged him who has so committed this, as though I were present. In the name of our Lord Jesus,

Paul was astonished that a member of the church could openly commit incest, and nothing would be done about it. How could this be? Worse still, how could the Corinthians apparently boast about their broad-minded acceptance of this Christian's immoral behaviour?

The brother needs correction, not cuddling, Paul tells them. He then earnestly enjoins them to remove the wicked man from their midst, to disas - sociate themselves from him and to refuse him any fellowship (v. 11, 13).

Why? - In order that his spirit might be saved (v. 5). The purpose of discipline is restoration, not simply retribution. And the Apostle also mentions his con - cern for the church's purity. The leaven of this man's sin had contaminated the Corinthians' char - acter and witness, which also needed to be restored by his removal (v. 6-8)

Fame and popularity are vanity. The only thing that endures is character. We are a church; a church of discipline.

Called to Forgive

Eager to obey Paul's advice, the Corinthians zeal-ously disciplined the wrongdoer, to the extent that, even after he confessed and repented of his sin, they still denied him fellowship in the church. This continued for about six months. The discipline accomplished its purpose. In his second letter to the Corinthians, Apostle Paul then called for a res-toration. It was now time to offer forgiveness and complete this believer's restoration to the body.

> *"This punishment which was inflicted by the majority is sufficient for such a man, so that, on the contrary, you ought rather to forgive and comfort him, lest perhaps such a one be swallowed up with too much sorrow. Therefore I urge you to reaffirm your love to him. For to this end I also wrote, that I might put you to the test, whether you are obedient in all things. Now whom you forgive anything, I also forgive. For if indeed I have forgiven anything, I have forgiven that one for your sakes in the presence of Christ, lest Satan should take advantage of us; for we are not ignorant of his devices."*
>
> *(2 Corinthians 2:6-11)*

Forgive, comfort, and reaffirm your love in beautiful balance. Paul exhorted the Corinthians to welcome back this repentant sinner with the same zealous intensity that characterised their enforcement of his discipline. He asked them to embrace the prodi-gal son and welcome him back home.

Where there has only been hurt, let it restore unity where there has only been division. Kill the fatted calf and celebrate! The importance of this forgiveness is underscored by Paul's caution in verse 11. Had the Corinthians continued withholding forgiveness from this man, ignoring his repentant attitude, Satan would have gained all the advantage he needed to cause him to despair.

Need to Repent

Later on in this same letter, Paul delineates the power of a repentant spirit.

> *"For godly sorrow worked repentance to salvation not to be repented of: but the sorrow of the world worked death."*
>
> *2 Corinthians 7:10*

This godly sorrow Paul focuses on is initiated by a humble and contrite heart, a heart open to the truth. This sorrow then produces change, a turning away from sin that is, in essence, what repentance means. This truth-driven change, in turn, leads the way to life-giving choices, since the truth is a "lamp unto [our] feet" that lights our way along the path of life (Psalm 119: 105). In summary, we could say that an open, receptive, vulnerable heart releases the power of God's truth because it invites Him in and makes a place for His presence in our lives.

The sorrow of the world, on the contrary, is not a sorrow that produces a desire to change. The only desire it generates is an urge to get rid of the painful consequences of sin, rather than a commitment to deal with the sinful choices that caused the pain in the first place. The heart of worldly sorrow is pride, too proud to admit the need of a Saviour. It is shut off to receiving the truth that would turn it toward life. So it traps itself in the unending ache of irredeemable regret, forever condemning itself to constant grief and hopelessness
(2 Corinthians 7:10b).

The truth of this verse can shed much light on Paul's plea for the Corinthians to forgive and restore their repentant brother. This man had come through sorrow, had opened himself to the truth and changed his course, and was now ready to re-enter the freedom and acceptance that Christ offers us all. The key lesson here is that, we should not get to the extreme and deny our brothers and sisters their place of forgiveness. But the Corinthians, in their earnest zeal to do right, were unwittingly blocking him from the path of life. They were prolonging his sorrow, his ache; what they needed to do was affirm his changed heart and their acceptance of him. This would be accomplished if they reached out to meet him in forgiveness.

"Therefore, as the elect of God, holy and beloved, put on tender mercies, kindness, humility, meekness, longsuffering; 13bearing with one another, and forgiving one another, if anyone has a complaint against another; even as Christ forgave you, so you also must do."

Colossians 3:12-13

"Now all things are of God, who has reconciled us to Himself through Jesus Christ, and has given us the ministry of reconciliation."

2 Corinthians 5:1

FORGIVING ONE ANOTHER

Basically, there are two roles in the forgiveness process: the role of the **offended** and that of the **offender**.

Now, let us focus on how a servant should respond when he or she is the offender.

When We Are the Offender

In a nutshell, *Matthew 5:23-24* describes the correct procedure to follow when we have offended someone.

"Therefore if you bring your gift to the altar, and there remember that your brother has something against you, leave your gift there before the altar, and go your way.

First be reconciled to your brother, and then come and offer your gift."

Matthew 5:23-24

The scene depicted in verse 23 is that of a worshipper in Jesus' days where animals were sacrificed for the forgiveness of sins. Imagine for a moment that this worshipper is you; you're at the altar, on your knees. What do you do when your conscience is suddenly pricked by the fact that you have offended someone?

Verse 24 outlines four steps:

1. Stop - "leave your offering there"

2. Go - go your way

3. Reconcile -"first be reconciled"

4. Return - "then come and present your offering"

The key term is reconciliation. It comes from a Greek verb meaning "to alter, to change," with a prefix added that means "through." They communicate the idea that we're to go through a process that will result in change. In other words, as the offender, we are to go and confess the wrong to the offended and seek forgiveness ideally, in person; if that's not possible, however, at least by phone or letter. Then we are free to return and worship God.

As simple as this process sounds, it is not always easy. Internal doubts and apprehensions can assail our minds and prevent us from carrying this process out. Let's face the usual "what if" and "what about" situations head-on.

1. **What if he or she refuses to forgive?**
   The important thing for each of us to remember is that each person is responsible for him/herself. With the right motive, in the right spirit, at the right time, out of obedience to God, we are to humble ourselves as servants and attempt to make things right. God will honour our efforts. The one offended may need time, first to get over the shock and next, to have God bring about a change in his or her heart. Healing sometimes takes time. It took Esau, over twenty years to let go of the pain Jacob had caused him.

2. **What if the situation gets worse?**
   This can happen. Naturally, the one offended feels bitter and keeps blaming the offender. Such a person could plan all kinds of evil; mentally sticking pins in your doll, hoping for a calamity to befall you. When you go to make peace, you suddenly cause his internal scales to go out of balance. You take away the blame and all that's left is the person's guilt. This could cause the person to have worse feelings.

3. **What if I decide to simply deal with it before God and not go through the pain and embarrassment of talking with the other person?**
   We'll do anything to make things easier, won't we? Well, first of all, that is a willful contradiction of the command.

Jesus says, "Stop, go, reconcile and return."Obeying this command helps prevent the situation from getting worse. Offended people tend to become wounded souls once they continue to harbour bitter feelings. If you have offended somebody, you have to reconcile with that person before you come to God.

> *Therefore if you bring your gift to the altar, and there remember that your brother has something against you, leave your gift there before the altar, and go your way. First be reconciled to your brother, and then come and offer your gift.*
>
> **Matthew 5:23-24**

...Forgiveness is the giving, and so the receiving, of life...

George MacDonald

10

THE DIABOLICAL NATURE
OF REVENGE

✳ ✳ ✳

A true story was told about a German army general who got badly wounded and lost a considerable amount of blood during world war two. Therefore, there was an urgent need for blood transfusion to save his life.

He was privileged to have a supply and the doctors rushed to work on him. With a fainting voice he asked, "Is that German blood or English blood?" "If this is English blood I will rather die than to mingle my blood with it." "English it is", answered one of the medical officers.

These doctors and nurses in astonishment had no choice but to let him have his will. Why will any man on earth deny himself of life? The reason is simple: this deadly sin called offence that breeds BITTERNESS.

Compassion is better than anger. Forgiveness is better than revenge. In deed his diabolic will was carried out and he died in a pool of blood. He lost his physical life and, without a shadow of doubt, his eternal life too.

According to the uncompromising word of God...

> *"For if you forgive men their trespasses, your heavenly Father will also forgive you."*
>
> **Mat 6:14.**

It's too late - Time has run out!

In her book "Divine Revelation of Hell," Rev. Mary Baxter revealed a true account of a woman of God who lost the power and grace to forgive her husband, who had cheated on her and blamed God for it. She moved from anger to resentment and to bitterness and finally to a cancer of hatred which led to murder.

She took the life of her husband, the life of the woman in question and her own life. She committed triple murder; the most painful part is that she lost her life eternally.

This heinous sin does not spare any personality, whether you are a Pope, an Archbishop, an Apostle, Prophet, Evangelist, Pastor or Teacher, President, Doctor, Lawyer, Engineer, Education Officer or a Human Relations Officer. This is the cardinal truth.

I am sure that, though her husband was murdered for unfaithfulness, he had eternal life. This is because there was no record of him in hell, as the wife pleaded with Jesus to give her another chance. The full account of this story is as follows:

This is Mary Baxter's trip to hell with the Lord Jesus Christ:

> "I listened as a woman speaks to Jesus from the flame of the pit. She was quoting the word of God, dear Lord, what is she doing here?" I asked.

> "Listen" Jesus said,

> The woman said, "Jesus is the Way the Truth and the Life. He is the Light of the world. Come to Him He will save you." When she spoke, many of the lost souls around listened. Some swore and cursed at her. Some told her to stop. Others said, "Is there really any hope?" "Help us Jesus." Great cries of sorrow filled the air.

> I didn't understand what was happening. I didn't know why the woman was preaching the gospel here.

> The Lord knew my thoughts. He said, "Child, I called this woman at the age of thirty to preach my Word and to be a witness of the gospel. I call different people for different purposes in My body. But any man or woman who does not want My Spirit I will depart from."

"Yes, she did answer My call for many years and she grew in the knowledge of the Lord. She learned My voice and she did many good works for Me. She studied the word of God, she prayed often, and she had many prayers answered. She taught many people the way of holiness and she was faithful in her house."

"The years went by until one day she found out that her husband was having an affair with another woman. Even though he asked for forgiveness, she grew bitter and would not forgive him and try to save her marriage. Truly her husband was wrong, and he had committed a grave sin."

"But this woman knew my word. She knew how to forgive; she knew that, for every temptation there is a way of escape. Her husband asked her to forgive him but she would not; instead anger took root and grew inside her. She would not turn over to Me. She turned bitter each day and said in her heart, 'Here I am serving God all the way, and my husband is running around with another woman! Do you think that is right?' She said to me."

"I said to her, 'No, it is not right. But he came to you and repented and said he would never do that again.'"

"I told her, 'Daughter, look inside of yourself, and see what you have caused to yourself.'"

A "Holier Than Thou" Attitude

"'Not me, Lord. I am the holy one and he is the sinful one,' she would not listen to Me. Time went on and she would not pray to Me or read the Bible. She became angry not only at her husband, but those around her, she quoted the scriptures, but she would not forgive him."

"She would not forgive him and not listen to Me. Her heart grew bitter, and a great sin entered in. Murder grew in her heart where love had once been. One day in her anger, she killed her husband and the other woman. Satan entered into her and took over completely and she killed herself afterwards."

I looked at that soul that had given up Christ and condemned her soul forever to the flame and the pain. "I will forgive now, Lord." She said. "I will obey you now, let me out. See Lord, I am preaching your word now. In an hour demons will come to take me and torment me, because I was preaching your word, my torment is worse. Please Lord, let me out."

Jesus said, "Time has run out for you!"

I cried with the woman in the pit and asked the Lord to please keep me from all bitterness of heart. "Don't let me allow hatred to come into my heart, Lord Jesus." I said.

Anyone, who refuses to forgive, is just like these two individuals who willingly chose to die rather than forgive their offenders. Life is worth living.

I Also Need To Be Loved

There are many untold stories out there that would blow your mind. I watched a talk show in the USA some years ago; a woman was invited to share her experience. Her own sister was sharing her husband with her.

The younger sister was married to this man and they had kids. Meanwhile the elder sister was also having an affair with him. The most disturbing part is that, she had also had two children with the same man.

She appeared on the show defending and justifying her actions. She was ready to fight her sister. A bitter conflict ensued between them.

When she was asked why she did such a vicious thing, her response was very outrageous. Not even bothered about the fact that she was live on television with millions of viewers watching and listening to her.

According to her, she could not understand the love and care the husband was showering onto the wife, her younger sister. She had never had that treatment and so vowed to continue to share the man with her sister for as long as she lived. This astonished the host of the show and the audience in the studio. There was no embarrassment, shame or even remorse on this woman's part.

She was not bothered at the hundreds of audiences at the studio who hooted at her and the shameless husband.

How could one expect the wife to forgive her sister, who was now her rival? This was obviously a very bitter situation. But for the real wife or the younger sister to walk in peace and calmness and enjoy her marriage, she needs to let go by the abounding grace of God.

For all you know, this younger sister might have offended the elder one in the past, for which she (the elder sister) had also decided to pay her back with such a shameful act.

Striving Without Cause

Many years ago, a friend, Akua, a dealer in women's clothes, narrated how a woman she had met, had shown irrational hostility towards her. She simply did not want to have anything to do with her, not even making eye contact.

This became such a concern to Akua, since she did not know what she had done to her to warrant such an attitude. Coincidentally, they bumped into each other at a friend's place and the woman did not hide her feeling of animosity towards Akua. This rancour toward her, made Akua very uncomfortable.

Since the woman refused to grant Akua any audience, she finally asked a friend of hers who knew this woman, to find out why the woman was behaving that way. Interestingly, the friend did not get any tangible reason from her. All she said was that, people can pick on you for no apparent reason and that should not be any cause for alarm.

Akua had a popular clothing design that was in vogue; everybody was looking for it. One fateful day, she received a phone call from a woman who also needed this design for an important occasion. Accordingly, Akua gave her direction to her house. The door bell rang so she hurried to open the door for this new customer. To her surprise, there stood this same woman who had been so hostile towards her. She had not recognised Akua's voice on the phone otherwise she would not have bothered herself. To say the least, she was so embarrassed by her own guilty conscience.

You need to imagine the scenario yourself. In this state of shock, she was invited and welcomed in. Akua went ahead to offer her a drink but she refused it, probably out of shame. The woman bought the clothing alright without any further discussion. She was given all the best attention to make her feel welcome and comfortable. It would not be a surprise if she never wore the clothing.

Akua caught a glimpse of her at a big conference of believers and was determined to greet her but the woman took the opposite direction when she saw her approaching.

> "If you have run with the footmen, and they have
> wearied you, Then how can you contend with horses?
> And if in the land of peace, In which you trusted, they

wearied you, Then how will you do in the floodplain of the Jordan?

Jeremiah 12:5

When things like these happen, let us ask the Lord Abba Father what He is trying to teach us. What lessons do we need to learn?

If you look at life the wrong way, there is always cause for alarm. What you see mainly depends on what you look for. Many people complain because roses have thorns but, beloved, let us be thankful to the Lord that thorns have roses.

If you cannot endure the gossip and lies, how can you stand in time of promotion? In the womb of adversity, champions are raised. All things work together for good, for those who are called of God.

Shattered Dreams

Another true story: A young lady and a young man had been in courtship for three years and were on the verge of making arrangements for their marriage. On the proposed day for their wedding, parents, relatives and friends had travelled from far and near to witness the occasion and lend their support. To the astonishment of all present, the man (supposed bridegroom) sent a 'last minute' message to the woman (supposed bride) that she should call off the marriage.

Every effort was made at convincing the young man to reconsider his decision and, at least, spare the bride and the dignitaries present any further embarrassment, but to no avail.

We don't need a rocket scientist to tell us the emotional and mental trauma the lady went through after the shame and disappointment. Her life was completely shattered.

To the young lady, this was an unresolved issue. Few months later, the young man was reported mentally ill and he had to be fired from his professional work. Today, he is confined to a mental institution.

The provident God who knows things before they happen had divinely intervened. **Provident** comes from the word *"provideo"* where *"pro"* means before and *"video"* means see. Who will enjoy marriage to a man or woman who becomes mentally disturbed just a couple of months after marriage?

Not every courtship guarantees marriage. Many have become so bitter at a man or woman who disappointed them in marriage. As a result, they are shattered in life. Faced with this situation, many people have done silly things as a form of revenge. When that happens, we walk by sight instead of faith.

What we fail to take note in such situations is that, the man or woman might not be the God-ordained husband or wife for you. God's omniscience and favour are working on your behalf, the Lord works in devices and ways beyond our human comprehension.

One of the greatest truths is that, when one door closes another opens. However, we often look so long and regretfully upon the closed door that we do not see the one that is open to us. Before the Lord will close one door, He would have already opened another. He doesn't only add or bring to you; He takes away and removes those who are a hindrance to His purpose and plan for your life. Let go so that you can lay hold. In His will is your peace.

If you can see God's hand in everything, you can leave everything in God's hand. If we will view things from Gods own perspective we will not be apprehensive. Paths without obstacles don't lead anywhere.

A dear sister and a friend minister preached a profound message on my husband's birthday. It was entitled, *"The hotter the fire the greater the deliverance."* Right from the fire, the three Hebrew men were promoted. No purification, no presentation. The harder the process, the finer the product. There is no short cut to maturity. God does not promote immature people.

> *"Take away the dross from silver, and it will go to the silversmith for jewelry."*
>
> **Proverbs 25:4**

As believers, it is important for us to see mishaps as God sees them, for His sovereign will cannot be hindered.

"I know that You can do everything, And that no purpose of Yours can be withheld (prevented) from You."

Job 42:2

...The weak can never forgive. Forgiveness is the attribute of the strong...

Mahatma Gandhi

11

SOME BIBLICAL LESSONS

* * *

Let us consider the life of Isaac. He is one of the prime examples of forgiveness. During a drought, he dug wells that his enemies moved in and claimed. Nevertheless, he did not retaliate; he moved on and dug new ones. God therefore blessed him and filled up his empty wells. God is still in the business of filling empty lives when we forgive those who have hurt us.

Jesus said in *John 15:1- 2*

> *I am the true vine, and my Father is the husbandman.*
> *Every branch in me that beareth not fruit he taketh*
> *away: and every branch that beareth fruit, he purgeth it,*
> *that it may bring forth more fruit.*

He also said in *Matthew 15:13*

> *But he answered and said, every plant, which my heavenly Father hath not planted, shall be rooted up.*

Anything that is not planted by the Father shall be cut off. The same thing will happen to anyone who comes to Jesus and does not bear fruit. He who belongs to Jesus was bought with a price and the Lord cleanses such a person. It is not an easy thing when you are going through difficulties in life, such as pain and suffering endured as a child of God. But if you cannot endure, then Jesus says you are none of His.

> *Nevertheless the foundation of God standeth sure, having this seal; The Lord knoweth them that are his. And, Let everyone that nameth the name of Christ depart from iniquity.*
>
> *2 Timothy 2:19*

The foundation stands sure. Nothing can move them. They will stand in times of storms, trials, temptations and tribulations. Because God has put them there and they are able to endure.

John the Baptist

The ministry of John the Baptist was defined even before he was born. He was coming to prepare the way for the Messiah. A time came that John was imprisoned. When he heard that Jesus was performing signs and wonders, he sent this message to Jesus:

> *And said unto him, Art thou he that should come, or*
> *do we look for another?*
>
> **Matthew 11:3**

He was expecting Jesus to come and deliver him from prison. The Bible says that John was offended because he was in prison. Whenever one becomes offended, the spirit leaves and the flesh takes over. The flesh does not give glory to God.

Every word that comes out of the flesh is negative. John became offended and bitter in prison and asked questions, *"Am I to wait for another or you are the one?"* He sounded unsure. The same man who not long ago said that Jesus was the Lamb of God is now asking if Jesus is really the Son of God. Why? Because he was offended and more so began to have doubts in his mind.

> *"Great peace has they which love thy law: and*
> *nothing shall offend them."*
>
> **Psalms 119:165**

Jesus replied John with the following message:

> *Jesus answered and said unto them, Go and show*
> *John again those things which ye do hear and see:*
> *the blind receive their sight, and the lame walk, the*
> *lepers are cleansed, and the deaf hear, the dead are*
> *raised up, and the poor have the gospel preached to*
> *them. And blessed is he, whosoever shall not be*
> *offended in me.*
>
> **Matthew 11:4-6**

The Bible says in *1 Corinthians 4:7*

> *For who maketh thee to differ from another? And what hast thou that thou didst not receive? Now if thou didst receive it, why dost thou glory, as if thou hadst not received it?*

What we forget is that, it is neither this brother nor that sister who died for us. It was Jesus who died for us and we are here because of Jesus. Why should you allow somebody to quench your spirit, quench the Spirit of the Living God and cease you from operating in the works and gifts of God? Jesus said that offences would come, but woe unto whosoever brings it. We have to be vigilant so that we can avoid being the sources of the offence. The devil does not want you to prosper in the spirit.

The Thief Cometh

> *"The thief cometh not, but for to steal, and to kill, and to destroy: I am come that they might have life, and that they might have it more abundantly."*
> **John 10:10**

> *"When any one heareth the word of the kingdom, and understandeth it not, then cometh the wicked one, and catcheth away that which was sown in his heart. This is he which received seed by the way side. But he that received the seed into stony places, the same is he that heareth the word, and anon with joy receiveth it; Yet hath he not root in himself, but dureth for a while: for*

*when tribulation or persecution ariseth because of the
word, by and by he is offended."*

Matthew 13:19-21

When one becomes born again or one hears the Word, a seed
is planted in the person. The seed is planted on a "ground" in
the heart. There are different types of grounds; stony ground,
rocky grounds, fertile, etc. The seeds that falls on the stony,
rocky grounds cannot germinate. Such hearts receive the
Word with joy and are zealous of the things of God. But all of
a sudden they drop out. In verse 21, it says that such people
have no root for the Word because they are offended when
persecution arises because of the Word.

They will not be able to stand when trials and temptations
come. So they would not allow the word of God to strengthen
and stabilise them. Many people have grown old in the
Church, yet they have not grown up spiritually. Emotional
hearers are usually not matured.

If you are grown up, when the time comes for tribulation and
trials, you are able to see it. Understand that the work that we
are doing in the house of the Lord is not to man, but to God.
Therefore if any man offends you, do not close up or withdraw
from the work. *Rev 3:11*

*Bondservants, be obedient to those who are your
masters according to the flesh, with fear and
trembling, in sincerity of heart, as to Christ;
6not with eyeservice, as men-pleasers, but as*

bondservants of Christ, doing the will of God from the heart, 7with goodwill doing service, as to the Lord, and not to men, 8knowing that whatever good anyone does, he will receive the same from the Lord, whether he is a slave or free.

Ephesians 6: 5-8

These things have I spoken unto you, that ye should not be offended. They shall put you out of the synagogues: yea, the time cometh, that whosoever killeth you will think that he doeth God service.

John 16:1-2

Let us look at how far offences can lead us to, and the lessons we can learn from these Biblical examples:

King Saul's Ordeal (1 Samuel 18-31)

In these chapters, we see how insecurity, evil and fear led King Saul to turn against a potential deliverer, David.

And it came to pass as they came, when David was returned from the slaughter of the Philistine, that the women came out of all cities of Israel, singing and dancing, to meet King Saul, with tablets, with joy, and with instruments of music. And the women answered one another as they played, and said, "Saul hath slain his thousands, and David his ten thousands." And Saul was very wroth, and the saying displeased him; and he said, they have ascribed unto David ten thousands, and to me they have ascribed but thousands:

and what can he have more but the kingdom? And Saul eyed David from that day and forward. And it came to pass on the morrow, that the evil spirit from God came upon Saul, and he prophesied in the midst of the house: and David played with his hand, as at other times: and there was a javelin in Saul's hand. And Saul cast the javelin; for he said, I will smite David even to the wall with it. And David avoided out of his presence twice.

1 Samuel 18:6-1

King Saul was offended because the women ascribed more praise to David than to him. He forgot that he did not fight in this battle. The Bible says that he was displeased. The word 'displeased' is the same as offended. And when he got offended, he started eyeing David. In Chapter 18 verse 10, it says that when Saul got offended, the spirit of the Lord left him and an evil spirit from the Lord came upon him.

Anytime one becomes offended he quenches and grieves the spirit of God, and closes the door of his heart to the spirit of God, doors open to evil spirits that takes over one's life.

Let every one of us consider the tendency of us falling as a prey to this trap of the devil. From the master to the servant, from the rich to the poor, from the white to the black, the list is endless.

Never underestimate the diabolic nature of an offence. The spirit of offence drives people away from the word of God because there is a possibility of change of heart when one hears the word of God. The harbouring of offences took Saul from wilderness to wilderness, chasing and trying to kill David. Offences and disobedience eventually drove Saul to his death. Bitterness is more devastating than betrayal.

> *Now the Philistines fought against Israel; and the men of Israel fled from before the Philistines, and fell slain on Mount Gilboa. 2Then the Philistines followed hard after Saul and his sons. And the Philistines killed Jonathan, Abinadab, and Malchishua, Saul's sons. 3The battle became fierce against Saul. The archers hit him, and he was severely wounded by the archers. 4Then Saul said to his armorbearer, "Draw your sword, and thrust me through with it, lest these uncircumcised men come and thrust me through and abuse me." But his armorbearer would not, for he was greatly afraid. Therefore Saul took a sword and fell on it.*

1 Samuel 31:1-4

Ahitophel's Story

In 2 Samuel chapter 13 to 17, the Bible talks about Ahitophel. He harboured offences in his heart because David had killed Uriah and had taken his wife, Bathsheba, who happened to be his granddaughter. He harboured this offence for years, waiting for the right opportunity for revenge. Yet he was a counsellor of

King David. The Bible says that when Ahitophel gave counsel it was like the oracles of God. Solomon was wise, but his wisdom was not as mature as that of Ahitophel.

Now David also had a son, but the child died because of the curse imposed on David at that time for killing Uriah and taking his wife.

GETTING EVEN - AN EYE FOR AN EYE

In *2 Samuel 13*, one of David's sons, Amnon, raped his own sister Tamah. Then Absalom also harboured that in his heart because his father didn't take any action against Amnon. He nurtured this offence in his heart for two years.

A time came that what he had harboured in his heart had to be made manifest. He plotted and killed his brother Amnon at a feast, after which he dashed away. But even in exile, he still had this offence in his heart. According to the Bible, he came back to Jerusalem and together with Ahitophel; they conspired against the king, David.

Ahitophel had the offence of Uriah at heart and Absalom also had the offence of Amnon at heart. They formed a confederacy and were able to draw and manipulate some of the people on their side and began to rebel against King David. Eventually, as their evil deeds began to back-fire, Ahitophel committed suicide by hanging himself.

Never be a victim of an offence. The deceiver can manipulate you to take your own life. Many lives have been shipwrecked due to this diabolic spirit; this spirit is more self inflicting than the offender.

Life is not as one desires it; it is filled with sharp corners and hard floors. We may try to cushion ourselves from the bumps and brace ourselves for the falls, pain and anguish, which are inescapable. We can't bury our heads in the sand like the ostrich and say there is nothing like offence. Neither can we hope that our faith will insulate as from the difficulties in life. This was not the case with the saints of old.

Doing Right and Suffering Wrong

God-fearing Joseph was sold into slavery by his brothers; he was falsely accused and imprisoned, and forgotten. Innocent Job was covered with skin ulcers and his friends called him names. Faithful Daniel was thrown into a lion's den. The tenacious John the Baptist was beheaded. Spirit-filled Stephen was stoned to death. Courageous Paul was beaten and almost stoned to death. Jesus Christ, the sinless son Of God, was crucified.

> Job rightly exclaimed "O man born of a woman is short lived and full of turmoil."
>
> **Job 14:1**

...To forgive is to set a prisoner free and discover the prisoner was you...

Anonymous

12

DOING RIGHT AND SUFFERING WRONG

✳ ✳ ✳

This topic is not an uncommon experience in life. A good number of people have encountered such situations. Let me lead you into a typical experience:

It was on a public holiday in May when I had a call from a woman and her sister who desperately wanted to see me. I made an appointment for us to meet in my house. The sister, who is resident in London, had a very pathetic story to share. According to her, she met this man who happened to be a porter at a hotel she lodged whiles on holidays in Ghana. He came around every day to offer his services to her. She then assigned him to run some errands for her.

When she was leaving for London, the man approached her and pleaded with the woman to take him on so he can work for her in London. Clearly, this man was finding life difficult and struggling to make ends meet. He had a family of six to fend for and to add to his despair, the whole family resided in one small room. So, you can imagine his situation.

Moved by his plight, the woman decided to help him. She had her own business running lucratively. According to her, she got every necessary document ready; obtained an employee's visa for him and they both came to London. The woman continued that she trained this man as an accountant and payroll officer and put him in charge of her business accounts.

In the long run, the man she had trusted and helped became very dishonest to her. He was paying people who did not exist; that is to say he filled the worksheet with ghost names. This he did for years and acquired his own properties. The man began to live affluently. Eventually, he was exposed and the woman fired him accordingly. As if that was not enough, on his departure, he took with him the floppy disk that contained the names of companies who owed his employer (the woman).

This woman tried every means to recover the information but to no avail. So she felt very bitter and decided to pay the man back 'in his own coin'. A friend of hers decided to assist by making an arrangement to woo this man to a meeting one Sunday morning, so she could unexpectedly appear there to demand her disk.

She vowed to eliminate this man upon meeting him, so she sharpened a knife and put it into her bag. The enemy entered into her. She told her only son about her plans and showed the knife to him that, in case she did not come back, he would know what to do. Not even the advice from her only son could make her change her mind. She was so bent on killing the man that she decided to keep vigil on the eve of the appointment in other not to waste time in the morning.

Why was she in my house telling me all that?
We run a Radio program at dawn on weekends and she had been a regular listener. In the early hours of Sunday, she was on her way to the bathroom when she heard this same voice she had been listening to, preaching on forgiveness. She said the message touched her heart instantly, particularly because it dwelt exactly on the bitterness in her heart. It sounded so direct and she was so overwhelmed that she called me a 'witch'.

I hit the hammer right on the nail, with the message: "Nobody is worth your blessing, comfort and breakthrough; many have ended up in institutions such as the prisons, mental homes and hospitals because they could not forgive, and some had lost dear lives. Let go and have your peace, joy and calmness. Don't put your dear life in anybody's hand to control"

I then mentioned the preacher in Divine Revelation of hell, who killed her husband, the mistress and then herself for his infidelity and ended up in hell. It hit her like a time bomb. She started considering her life and the probable consequence of her intended action.

She began to contemplate: supposing she meets this man and tries to stab him and he ends up putting up a fight, anything could happen. Any of them could have been severely injured, and ended up in the hospital or in prison. To this stunning reality, she began to cry, threw herself on her bed and sobbed for hours. Finally, she decided to forgive the man. Interestingly, her friend who had made the arrangements insisted she come and meet this man but she turned it down.

The reality dawned on her that she could have been languishing in prison, if she had gone ahead with her plan. Incidentally, her company supplies workers to such institutions; prisons and hospitals. With some aura of relief and gladness in her heart, she said, "I have a cherub of one thousand pounds for you for saving my life from prison or death." This is a woman of substance whose testimony transforms many lives any time I share it.

The Biblical Account

Joseph

Joseph is given much prominence in the Bible from Genesis chapter 37 to chapter 50 also paints a vivid picture of a man with a forgiving spirit. After all the needless suffering his brothers put him through, he forgave them. The Good Lord rewarded him accordingly.

This loving son became the hated brother. His brothers hated him because his father loved him and because he had dreams. They hated him so much that they planned to end his life. His dream therefore became a nightmare. They sold him to the

Ishmaelites and he ended up in Potiphar's house. Here again, he was falsely accused of raping his master's wife. This took him to prison; a typical case of doing right and suffering wrong. In prison, he interpreted dreams for a baker and the king's cupbearer. One of them also forgot him. He therefore remained in prison. But there was not a single place in the Bible where it was recorded that Joseph held resentment or bitterness against anybody, be it his brothers, Potiphar's wife or the king's cupbearer. Even when his brothers finally came to Egypt, he joyfully received them.

He told them:

> *"... Do not be afraid, for am I in the place of God? But as for you, you meant evil against me; but God meant it for good, in order to bring it about as it is this day, to save many people alive. Now therefore, do not be afraid; I will provide for you and your little ones." And he comforted them and spoke kindly to them."*
>
> *Genesis 50: 19-21*

Joseph is a type of Christ. When we criticise we become like ordinary men, when we fight we become like animals; when we forgive, we become like God. Forgiveness is the nature of God.

> *"This punishment which was inflicted by the majority is sufficient for such a man, so that, on the contrary, you ought rather to forgive and comfort him, lest perhaps such a one be swallowed up with too much sorrow. Therefore I urge you to reaffirm your love to him."*
>
> *2 Corinthians 2:6-8*

The ten brothers knew that they were guilty, so they could not forgive themselves. That is the problem with most of us. Many cannot forgive themselves of some things they did against others and themselves.

Such people keep blaming themselves or others for their mishaps in life. All one needs to do is to repent and he or she will be forgiven. Guilt can hold one captive.
He told them:

> "If we confess our sins, he is faithful and just to forgive us our sins, and to cleanse us from all unrighteousness."
> *1 John 1:9*

David

Let us look at the account of David. This young man was anointed king of Israel at a very tender age but his crown was still on the head of his adversary, King Saul. What could he have done to get it?

King Saul hated David right from the beginning when he was anointed king. He tried to kill David on several occasions. He even went to the extent of killing eighty-five priests because they helped David to escape *(1 Samuel 18:5-11)*.

In *Chapters 21;10-15* of 1st Samuel, David dressed like a mad man and ran into the camp of the Philistines, Israel's archenemy at the time. Imagine an anointed king running from cave to cave in the wilderness looking for refuge. He was sought after like a wounded deer leaving traces of blood. Saul also left the palace and went into the wilderness to get David killed.

David had to stay in the wilderness with his entire family, and thus mingling with bandits and outcasts, those who were in distress.

> *"And everyone who was in distress, everyone who was in debt, and everyone who was discontented gathered to him. So he became captain over them. And there were about four hundred men with him."*
>
> **1 Samuel 22: 2-19**

The Bible says David did not desire to kill King Saul. He had the chance on two occasions to kill Saul, yet he touched him not because he considered Saul to be God's anointed *(1 Samuel 24: 6)*. He left everything into the hands of God. Even he ordered the execution of the Amelikite who claimed to be responsible for killing King Saul. When he heard that Saul had died, he lamented.

> *"Therefore David took hold of his own clothes and tore them, and so did all the men who were with him. 12And they mourned and wept and fasted until evening for Saul and for Jonathan his son, for the people of the LORD and for the house of Israel, because they had fallen by the sword. 13Then David said to the young man who told him, "Where are you from?" And he answered, "I am the son of an alien, an Amale-kite." 14So David said to him, "How was it you were not afraid to put forth your hand to destroy the LORD'S anointed?" 15Then David called one of the young men and said, "Go near, and execute him!" And he struck him so that he died. 16So David said to him,*

and said, "Go near, and execute him!" And he struck him so that he died. 16So David said to him, "Your blood is on your own head, for your own mouth has testified against you, saying, 'I have killed the LORD'S anointed.'"

2 Samuel 1: 11-16

"Then David lamented with this lamentation over Saul and over Jonathan his son, 18and he told them to teach the children of Judah the Song of the Bow; indeed it is written in the Book of Jasher: 19"The beauty of Israel is slain on your high places! How the mighty have fallen! 20Tell it not in Gath, Proclaim it not in the streets of Ashkelon--Lest the daughters of the Philistines rejoice, Lest the daughters of the uncircumcised triumph. 21"O mountains of Gilboa, Let there be no dew nor rain upon you, Nor fields of offerings. For the shield of the mighty is cast away there! The shield of Saul, not anointed with oil. 22From the blood of the slain, From the fat of the mighty, The bow of Jonathan did not turn back, And the sword of Saul did not return empty. 23"Saul and Jonathan were beloved and pleasant in their lives, And in their death they were not divided; They were swifter than eagles, They were stronger than lions. 24"O daughters of Israel, weep over Saul, Who clothed you in scarlet, with luxury; Who put ornaments of gold on your apparel. 25"How the mighty have fallen in the midst of the battle! Jonathan was slain in your high places. 26I am distressed for you, my brother Jonathan;

> *You have been very pleasant to me; Your love to me was wonder-*
> *ful, Surpassing the love of women. 27"How the mighty have*
> *fallen, And the weapons of war perished!"*
>
> *2 Samuel 1: 17-27*

He forbade the people not to publish the death of Saul, lest their enemies hear of it and rejoice about the calamity of King Saul. It takes a man with a forgiving spirit to go this far with someone who had been such a thorn in his flesh and a source of torment for him.

> *"Tell it not in Gath, Proclaim it not in the streets of Ashkelon--Lest*
> *the daughters of the Philistines rejoice, Lest the daughters of the*
> *uncircumcised triumph."*
>
> *2 Samuel 1: 20*
>
> *"13Then David said to the young man who told him, "Where are*
> *you from?" And he answered, "I am the son of an alien, an*
> *Amalekite." 14So David said to him, "How was it you were not*
> *afraid to put forth your hand to destroy the LORD'S anointed?"*
> *15Then David called one of the young men and said, "Go near,*
> *and execute him!" And he struck him so that he died. 16So David*
> *said to him, "Your blood is on your own head, for your own*
> *mouth has testified against you, saying, 'I have killed the LORD'S*
> *anointed."*
>
> *2 Samuel 1: 13-16*

Not only that, David also cursed the mountain on which Saul and his sons died.

> *You have been very pleasant to me; Your love to me was wonder-*
> *ful, Surpassing the love of women. 27"How the mighty have*
> *fallen, And the weapons of war perished!"*
>
> *2 Samuel 1: 17-27*

And up to today, according to scientists, not even a string of grass has grown on that mountain. When he heard that the people of Jabesh-Gilead were the ones who buried Saul, he went to them and poured blessings upon them.

> *"And the men of Judah came, and there they anointed David king*
> *over the house of Judah. And they told David, saying, that the*
> *men of Jabeshgilead were they that buried Saul. And David sent*
> *messengers to the men of Jabeshgilead, and said unto them,*
> *blessed be you of the LORD, that you have shewed this kindness*
> *to your lord, even unto Saul, and have buried him."*
>
> *2 Samuel 2: 4-5*

Let us emulate the examples of David and Joseph for what they did. The Bible says that we should pray for our enemies, we should forgive them and if they are hungry we should feed them.

By so doing, you heap coals of fire upon their head. *Romans 12: 20*

"Let all bitterness, and wrath, and anger, and clamour, and evil speaking, be put away from you, with all malice: And be ye kind one to another, tenderhearted, forgiving one another, even as God for Christ's sake hath forgiven you."

Ephesians 4:31-32

"Do not devise evil against your neighbor, For he dwells by you for safety's sake. Do not strive with a man without cause, If he has done you no harm. Do not envy the oppressor, And choose none of his ways."

Proverbs 3: 29-31

WHY DOES THE RIGHTEOUS SUFFER?

Job

Job held resentment against his three friends who came up to him during his suffering and affliction. This is because they did not comfort him but rather added more injuries to his wounds. They called him all kinds of names. This is affirmed in *Chapter 8:13*

"So are the paths of all who forget God; And the hope of the hypocrite shall perish",

His friends called him a hypocrite, a sinner. They wrongly under-stood Job's situation and rather attributed his calamities to his sins. Another friend said *"Is not your wickedness great,*

And your iniquity without end?" (Chapter 22: 5). But the Bible says that he was a perfect upright man and eschewed evil. He was a man of integrity. Due to these unkind words, Job held resentment against these friends until he had a revelation that if he did not pray for these friends, the Lord would not heal him.

> *"And the LORD turned the captivity of Job, when he prayed for*
> *his friends: also the LORD gave Job twice as much as he had*
> *before."*
>
> ***Job 42:10***

When we forgive, we get deliverance, restoration, Joy, peace and abundance comes upon us.

Let us look at New Testament examples:

Stephen

Stephen was a young deacon who stood up to defend the faith, for which he was stoned to death.

> *"And said, Behold, I see the heavens opened, and the Son of man*
> *standing on the right hand of God."*
>
> ***Acts 7:56***
>
> *"And they stoned Stephen, calling upon God, and saying, Lord*
> *Jesus, receive my spirit. And he kneeled down, and cried with a*
> *loud voice, Lord; lay not this sin to their charge. And when he had*
> *said this, he fell asleep."*
>
> ***Acts 7:59-60***

He could have died cursing his killers but he asked the Lord not to hold it against them. It is the only place in the Bible that it is recorded that Jesus stood on the right hand of God. Every other place records Jesus as sitting on the right hand of God. Because of the forgiving spirit in Stephen's life, he saw Jesus standing and ushering him into heaven. This is a mark of honour; to cause the Lord Jesus Christ to stand for you. I pray for all who read this book to emulate this example.

Our Lord Jesus Christ

He was crucified without cause but he asked for forgiveness for those who maltreated Him:

> "But he was wounded for our transgressions; he was bruised for our iniquities: the chastisement of our peace was upon him; and with his stripes we are healed. All we like sheep have gone astray; we have turned everyone to his own way; and the LORD hath laid on him the iniquity of us all. He was oppressed, and he was afflicted, yet he opened not his mouth: he is brought as a lamb to the slaughter, and as a sheep before her shearers is dumb, so he opened not his mouth. He was taken from prison and from judgment: and who shall declare his generation? For he was cut off out of the land of the living: for the transgression of my people was he stricken. And he made his grave with the wicked and with the rich in his death; because he had done no violence, neither was any deceit in his mouth. Yet it pleased the LORD to bruise him; he hath put him to grief: when thou shalt make

his soul an offering for sin, he shall see his seed, he shall prolong his days, and the pleasure of the LORD shall prosper in his hand. He shall see of the travail of his soul, and shall be satisfied: by his knowledge shall my righteous servant justify many; for he shall bear their iniquities. Therefore will I divide him a portion with the great, and he shall divide the spoil with the strong; because he hath poured out his soul unto death: and he was numbered with the transgressors; and he bare the sin of many, and made intercession for the transgressors."

Isaiah 53:5-12

Another refreshing example is that, even on the cross, in the midst of torture, Jesus promised the thief that he will be with Him in paradise.

"Then said Jesus, Father, forgive them; for they know not what they do. And they parted his raiment, and cast lots."

Luke 23:34

"When you hold resentment toward another, you are bound to that person or condition by an emotional link that is stronger than steel. Forgiveness is the only way to dissolve that link and get free."

Catherine Ponder

13

THE ANALOGY OF THE FORGIVING GOD

✳ ✳ ✳

B ELOW is the analogy of the forgiving God and the sinful human nature. This analogy was given by the Lord Himself as a parable unto His disciples.

Therefore the kingdom of heaven is like a certain king who wanted to settle accounts with his servants. And when he had begun to settle accounts, one was brought to him who owed him ten thousand talents. But as he was not able to pay, his master commanded that he be sold, with his wife and children and all that he had, and that payment be made. The servant therefore fell down before him, saying, 'Master, have patience with me, and I will pay you all.' Then the master of that servant was moved with compassion, released him, and forgave him the debt.

Matthew 18: 23-27

The above parable is a perfect example that the Lord gave to the disciples. The Almighty God has forgiven humanity so much. How then can't we forgive the little sins others commit against us. The Lord used the word "talent" which has great value. It was not an ordinary sum of money. It was a tribute used to pay kings and queens in those days. In our days, it could be millions of dollars or British pounds. Let us consider the clemency the master exhibited on this servant.

> *"Then the master of that servant was moved with compassion, released him, and forgave him the debt."*
>
> *Matthew 18: 27*

To release him means that he was previously holding that servant in bondage. When you have resentment, anger and bitterness against somebody, what it implies is that you hold that person and yourself in bondage or slavery. This is because when you see that person, your heart beats faster. You feel the acid in you and this acid burns. It makes you and that person uncomfortable. Why should you torment yourself?

Because the above servant could not pay, the Lord set him free. Let us put ourselves in the place of this servant and start counting the sins we have committed. We will see that we owe the Lord so much, but He has forgiven us. That is why you are born again. If it has not been the forgiving spirit of the Lord, none of us would have survived by now. We do not deserve to be forgiven, but by His grace, He chose to forgive us. We are saved.

"For by grace you have been saved through faith, and that not of yourselves; it is the gift of God, not of works, lest anyone should boast."

Ephes. 2:8-9

By His grace, we have been forgiven. This means we need to forgive one another. The servant in the above parable was forgiven and freed. Even though he was given enough time to pay the debt but he could not. This is because it was a huge debt. He didn't even make the attempt to pay this debt until he was arrested.

Our conscience always draws our attention to whatever wrong we do. It forces us to give account of what we are doing. It is the policeman of our soul and spirit.

The servant was forgiven and freed. But what happened next was even more interesting.

"But the same servant went out, and found one of his fellow servants, which owed him an hundred pence: and he laid hands on him, and took him by the throat, saying, Pay me that thou owes. And his fellow servant fell down at his feet, and besought him, saying, Have patience with me, and I will pay thee all. And he would not: but went and cast him into prison, till he should pay the debt."

Matthew 18: 28-30

This servant was demanding justice, which he was not qualified for. Interestingly, after he had been forgiven of his huge debt, he fiercely refused to show that kind gesture to a fellow brother. This is the situation in which most of us find ourselves.

> *"Blessed are the merciful: for they shall obtain mercy."*
>
> **Matthew 5: 7**

If one does not forgive, he or she shouldn't ask for mercy or even expect it.

> *"And whenever you stand praying, if you have anything against anyone, forgive him, that your Father in heaven may also forgive you your trespasses. But if you do not forgive, neither will your Father in heaven forgive your trespasses."*
>
> **Mark 11: 25-26**

One cannot commune with the Holy God with resentment and unforgiving spirit in his or her heart. "He is holy and He expects us to be holy too" (1 Peter 1:16). This servant went to demand something of which he had previously been forgiven, but much more in value. He went to demand cents and pence from his fellow servant, when he had just moments ago been forgiven of his debt of millions of pounds or dollars. He did not heed to the plea of his fellow servant for time to pay this debt.

> *"So his fellow servant fell down at his feet and begged him, saying, 'Have patience with me, and I will pay you all.*

"And he would not, but went and threw him into prison till he should pay the debt".

Matthew 18: 29-30

So much has been forgiven us than what we claim had been done against us. It is in this vein that we must show mercy and compassion towards each other.

The man who broke the wall of the bridge of forgiveness forgot that one day he will need to travel on it.

"And whenever you stand praying, if you have anything against anyone, forgive him, that your Father in heaven may also forgive you your trespasses. But if you do not forgive, neither will your Father in heaven forgive your trespasses."

Mark 11: 25-26

I am yet to see a man who can consciously inflict wounds on his own body and even hate his own soul. We need to emulate what the Lord did. That is why we are called kingdom children; we have dominion to overcome this ploy of the enemy. The early Church members were called Christians because they behaved and led Christ-like life. A Christian must have a testimony, a forgiving life.

"For whatever things were written before were written for our learning, that we through the patience and comfort of the Scriptures might have hope".

Romans 15: 4

We have been forgiven so much. What is stopping us from forgiving a brother or sister? It could be pride, self-centeredness and high self esteemed. That is why we find it difficult to forgive.

> *"And his lord was wroth, and delivered him to the tormentors, till he should pay all that was due to him."*
>
> *Matthew 18:34*

I don't think we will be able to handle it, if the gracious God decides to hand us over to tormentors; will you be able to bear it? If one cannot forgive, that person is telling the Lord to treat him the way he treats his fellow neighbour. If you go before the Lord with an unforgiving heart, you are wasting your time.

> *"If I regard iniquity in my heart, The Lord will not hear."*
>
> *Psalm 66:18*

> *"But we are all like an unclean thing, And all our righteousnesses are like filthy rags; We all fade as a leaf, And our iniquities, like the wind, Have taken us away."*
>
> *Isaiah 64:6*

It is wrong to condemn one another on the grounds of righteousness.

> *"Judge not, and you shall not be judged. Condemn not, and you shall not be condemned. Forgive, and you will be forgiven."*
>
> *Luke 6: 37*

> *"For to this you were called, because Christ also suffered for us, leaving us an example, that you should follow His steps,"*
>
> *1 Peter 2: 21*

Forgive, that you will be forgiven. Forgive. Beloved, we are doing so much evil to ourselves. We are blocking our blessings. The accuser of the brethren is always accusing you before the Lord even as you go before the Lord to pray.

Satan keeps reminding the Lord of the resentment you have against your neighbour. Unforgiving spirit is what the Lord cannot stand. Because He has forgiven us so much and He expects us to do likewise to others. The Bible says that the prayers of the wicked are an abomination unto the Lord.

> *"The sacrifice of the wicked is an abomination to the LORD, But the prayer of the upright is His delight. The way of the wicked is an abomination to the LORD, But He loves him who follows righteousness".*
>
> **Proverbs 15: 8-9**

During his missionary tour in the American colonies, John Wesley had a problem with a General called James Oglethorpe. He was known for his pride, harshness and wickedness. The General was so harsh that no man could stand before him. One day he declared, "I never forgive." Then, John Wesley said to him, "Sir, I hope you will never sin". Mahatma Gandhi once said to some Christians who were trying to convert him,

"I like your Christ, but I do not like you Christians because you are not like Christ. Your Christ has a forgiving spirit, but not you. So you cannot convert me." The lesson here is that, Christians should be careful not to become stumbling blocks.

When we go back to the parable, the Bible says:

> *And his master was angry, and delivered him to the torturers until he should pay all that was due to him.*
> **Matthew 18: 34**

Is this not fair? Of course it is. We have been forgiven of the millions of debts that we owed, but we refuse to forgive somebody of the "fifty pence" that he owes us.

The spirit of unforgiveness will eat away your peace and take your calmness from you. One cannot pray with this sin in his heart, otherwise it will amount to hypocrisy. As a child of God, you should go empty in yourself when you pray, not holding anything against someone. That heaviness is your inability to pray at that moment, something holds you from going to communicate with God. For the Lord deals with one's heart first. If you do not have this spirit of forgiveness, I urge you to pray for grace.

Let us see what God does unto us when we do not forgive:

> *"So My heavenly Father also will do to you if each of you,*
>
> *from his heart, does not forgive his brother his trespasses."*

Matthew 18: 35.

If you do not forgive, do not expect to be forgiven. Our heavenly Father will treat you the same way that you treat your brothers and sisters. This is a Biblical principle. You are telling the Lord, "Do unto me as I do unto others." We should usually ask ourselves how much we owe the Lord. When we do, we will realise that we have a lot of forgiveness to ask for. It is only when we forgive our brothers and sisters that we can rest in the bosom of the Father with the peace and calmness in our hearts.

Vengeance is the Lord's

Christ said that we should follow His steps. He suffered and left an example. He did not retaliate or reply. For instance, as the King of kings, he had the power to retaliate but he didn' t. Rather, He left an example for us to follow. This is the purpose for which we have been called, to forgive one another so that we might be blessed.

> *"Not rendering evil for evil, or railing for railing: but contra-*
>
> *riwise blessing; knowing that ye are thereunto called, that ye*
>
> *should inherit a blessing."*

1 Peter 3: 9

Why are pastors fighting against each other and churches against churches? Is Christ divided? We are one body, one baptism, one spirit and one faith. We should be aware of the devices of the enemy.

Submit yourselves therefore to God. Resist the devil, and he will flee from you.

James 4: 7

"Now whom you forgive anything, I also forgive. For if indeed I have forgiven anything, I have forgiven that one for your sakes in the presence of Christ, lest Satan should take advantage of us; for we are not ignorant of his devices."

2 Corinthians 2: 10-11

Do not let the devil take advantage of you. When you give him a field day, he takes advantage of it. It is a spirit the devil capitalises on against the people of God, because it is part of our lives. We can't forgive. The fact that you forgive does not mean God forgives the person:

"Dearly beloved, avenge not yourselves, but rather give place unto wrath: for it is written, Vengeance is mine; I will repay, says the Lord."

Romans 12: 19- 21

When you forgive, hand it over to the Creator. All powers belong to Him. You cannot give the person the merit that he or she deserves. You will make a mess of it. God knows what He is doing. He works it out in His own way. If you know how to fight your battles, the Lord will not fight for you. Many have been bruised, hurt, neglected and disappointed, but you have no right to reply or to hold it. The Bible says no! Consider the clemency that is granted unto you by the merciful and compassionate God and show same to others.

Forgiveness is . . . accepting God's sovereign use of people and situations to strip you of self importance, and humiliate your self love...

Martha Kilpatrick

14

GOD HAS A GREATER PLAN FOR YOU

* * *

PRECIOUS one, some of these offences hurt but the Lord allows them to come our way to test us, to teach us and to toughen us for elevation. When a man fails a test under no circumstances, will he be promoted? Many want promotion without examination. Triumph without trials. Testimony without test. God will not elevate you to any place He has not equally prepared you for.

Again, God uses these circumstances and situations to disassociate us from some people who have been stigmas and have retarded our progress in lives. The Lord allows us to go through these situations to sever us from others. And this allows us to focus and clearly hear from Him.

Prayer of Confession

God has a greater plan for you and so you don't have to entertain bitterness because it blocks Heaven's gate. When someone hurts or offends us, God commnands us to forgive. You may understand it one day or never why you need to forgive. Beloved one thing I am certain about is for you to forgive whoever has offended you, for your own sake and to be able to move on.

Make this confession (call names both the living and the dead). Some of them you need to go personally, and settle matters with them. Phone calls or letters can ease off pains in some people.

> *I forgive my parents (mother and father), husband, wife, ex-husband, ex-wife, brothers, sisters, sons, daughters for lack of love, affection and tenderness, my in-laws, for interfering in our family, school teachers who punished me unjustly, employers, co-workers who harassed and made life so miserable for me or lied about me.*

> *I forgive my ministers, elders, and brethren, friends who betrayed and denied me, neighbours who treated me so badly, now I also ask forgiveness from all those whom I have hurt, both the living and the dead.*

Please pray this prayer for strength and the grace to forgive and to be forgiven.

Heavenly father, I come before your throne this moment, haven read this cardinal truth, I surrender totally to you, my hurts and wounds and receive Your healing, deliverance, restoration, joy and peace right now in the name of JESUS CHRIST, THE SON OF THE LIVING GOD. Amen.

Forgiveness is the only attribute that distinguishes us from the world; it is the spirit of Christ.

Love is the only irresistible appeal we can offer to the disturbed, wounded, broken and decaying world.

In celebration of God's forgiveness towards us, let us be first to forgive.

Love is lacking in our mist. We, His Kingdom citizens, know much about God's attributes and so it is imperative for us to know and understand His love.

"For this is the message that you heard from the beginning, that we should love one another."

1 John 3:11

The poem of Love.

"Love is patient and kind; love is not jealous or boastful; 5it is not arrogant or rude. Love does not insist on its own way; it is not irritable or resentful; 6it does not rejoice at wrong, but rejoices in the right. 7Love bears all things, believes all things, hopes all things, endures all things."

1 Corinthians 13:4-7 RSV

USEFUL BIBLE VERSES

These are some practical verses that you can meditate upon:

Isaiah 61:1-7,
The Spirit of the Lord GOD is upon me; because the LORD hath anointed me to preach good tidings unto the meek; he hath sent me to bind up the brokenhearted, to proclaim liberty to the captives, and the opening of the prison to them that are bound; To proclaim the acceptable year of the LORD, and the day of vengeance of our God; to comfort all that mourn; To appoint unto them that mourn in Zion, to give unto them beauty for ashes, the oil of joy for mourning, the garment of praise for the spirit of heaviness; that they might be called trees of righteousness, the planting of the LORD, that he might be glorified. And they shall build the old wastes, they shall rise up the former desolations, and they shall repair the waste cities, the desolations of many generations. For your shame ye shall have double; and for confusion they shall rejoice in their portion: therefore in their land they shall possess the double: everlasting joy shall be unto them.

Psalm 30:5,
For his anger endures but a moment; in his favour is life: weeping may endure for a night, but joy comes in the morning.

Psalm 107:20,
He sent his word, and healed them, and delivered them from their destructions.

Psalm 147:3,
He heals the broken in heart, and binds up their wounds.

Isaiah 60:15,
Whereas thou hast been forsaken and hated, so that no man went through you, I will make thee an eternal Excellency, a joy of many generations.

Jeremiah 30:17,
For I will restore health to you, and I will heal you of your wounds, says the LORD; because they called thee an outcast, saying, this is Zion, whom no man seeketh after.

Malachi 4:2,
But to you that fear my name shall the Sun of righteousness arise with healing in his wings; and you shall go forth, and grow up as calves of the stall.

Luke 17:3,
Take heed to yourselves: If your brother trespass against thee, rebuke him; and if he repent, forgive him.

Acts 10:38,

How God anointed Jesus of Nazareth with the Holy Ghost and with power: who went about doing well, and healing all that were oppressed of the devil; for God was with him.

Col. 3:13,

Forbearing one another and forgiving one another, if any man has a quarrel against any: even as Christ forgave you, so also do ye.